THE RING FORMULA:

How to be the Only *One* He Ever Needs

Dr. Alduan Tartt

The Secret to Getting Men to Approach, Court, Commit, and Marry **YOU**.

Unattributed quotations are by Dr. Alduan Tartt

Edition ISBN's

Softcover	978-0-9817309-2-9
Hardcover	978-0-9817309-3-6
E-Book	

Second edition 2010.
10 9 8 7 6 5 4 3 2

Printed in the United States of America.

Book edited by Dr. Valerie Matthews Dotson (vdotson@gpc.edu)

THE RING FORMULA
How To Be The Only One He Ever Needs
Visionary Minds, Inc. Publishing
160 Clairemont Ave., Ste 200
Atlanta, GA 30030 U.S.A.

ISBN 978-0-9817309-2-9
LCCN 2010939748

CONTENTS

Why spend precious time worrying about whether you will ever get or stay married, when you can be working towards it right now?

Preface

Note to the Reader

This is a book geared towards women who wish to marry or stay married and desire a greater understanding of what it takes for good men to place and keep a wedding ring on their fingers.

Before writing this book, I had the impression that such information was routinely passed along from married fathers and mothers to their daughters; however, I quickly discovered that conversations about how to court men towards marriage were no longer commonplace.

As a result, an increasing number of talented, gorgeous and available women are currently dating without a ring formula for marriage. Men are simple creatures but do have complex needs. Learning how to meet them will place you on the fast track to establishing a foundation for marriage. By contrast, having a poor understanding of men's needs will inevitably lead to unnecessary confusion, conflict, divorce, and heartache.

The most important key is to love yourself so that men can provide you with the lifelong commitment, love, and respect you deserve. I invite you to read this book in one day and apply the principles to your current relationships.

As you read, remember that dating to marry is very different from regular dating because it requires you to be that "total package" that all men want in a wife. While pretty women are a dime a dozen, total packages possess the skill and knowledge to care masterfully for the needs of their men like no other. Become that total package, and the men will flock to you in droves. Why? Because the number one reason men give for not getting married is the inability to find the ONE, the total package that all men require in a wife.

Before you begin, prepare to have fun, laugh, and think seriously about bringing your total package at all times. My aim is genuinely to express what men look for in a wife so that women worldwide are equipped to successfully date towards and preserve marriage.

This is not a book for women who are convinced of men's inherent evil or have resigned themselves to a lifetime of loneliness. It is, however, for women who may have been hurt, discouraged, or never been told how beautiful they truly are. I will continue to pray that God allows these words of advice to empower you to blossom into the dynamic woman God created you to be and find the man of your dreams. Instead, this is a book for women who refuse to take NO for an answer. While you accept that no one is perfect, you are convinced that you are the perfect match for your MR. RIGHT and deserve to be on the fast track to monogamy, marriage, and children.

Consider this book your inspirational survival guide to dating towards marriage. I'm going to unmask men to you so that you can clearly see just how much they truly do need you regardless of what they say. Get ready as I reveal the RING FORMULA for marrying the man of your dreams.

It's now OK to pull out those wedding magazines and visit your favorite florist and jeweler because this book is going to guide you toward being the only one he ever needs.

Sincerely,

Alduan Tartt, Ph.D.

Acknowledgements

I would like to thank all the amazing people who supported and encouraged me throughout writing this wonderful book. First, I want to thank God for giving me the words, faith, and perseverance when Alduan, and especially Dr. Tartt, simply ran out. Thanks to my mom, dad, and brother who always support all of the ideas I have, no matter how unrealistic they may initially seem. Thanks for editing repeatedly and your unconditional love.

Thanks to Ellie Wharton (2lifepublications.com) for guiding me through the book writing process and making my work so much better. Thanks to Alvin Jackson, James Marshall Dixon, and especially Johanna Anderson for expanding and promoting my vision in the initial stages. Thanks to Kay duPont for the initial editing of this book and the encouragement. Thanks to Dr. Valerie Matthews Dotson (vdotson@gpc.edu) and Val Hunt for final editing of the book. Special thanks to Letitia Owens (rtishcreations.com) for her godly spirit that helped me see my calling. Thanks to Ilia Leathers (inikcokreative.com) for packaging such a stunning book cover.

Special thanks to all the phenomenal people who shared their time and talents with me to help me to better understand women. Thanks Mom, Dad, Sean, Pam, Harriet, Kimberly, Yohance, Kim, Melanie, Evonya, Hycine, Valerie, Charlene, Nicole, Erika, Vernicia, Latoya, Bree, Tammy, Jamila, Shani, Lynnette, Pam, Irma, Rachel, Alena, Kisalyn, Lauren, Yvonne, Rajah, Tabitha, Bridgette, Nina, Bessie, Anedra, Natasha, Joy, Nicole, Valdoshia Hunt, and Mecca.

Introduction

Ask Men (not Women) for Advice About Men

"Completing a test is always easier when you have the key in front of you." While men will openly admit that they don't understand women, far too many women make the unfortunate mistake of overestimating their overall knowledge about men. As men, we must take partial responsibility for being frequently misunderstood because rarely do we unmask and tell you what and how we truly feel. In fact, we really expect you to know already how we feel, how to meet our needs and why we need you. After all, mama seemed to intuitively know these things.

While this seems illogical, it is true and unfortunately makes dating us very confusing, frustrating and stressful. Tell you something you don't already know, right! Well God is good and always offers opportunities to serve. So, being a servant, I decided to be part of the solution by telling you everything (well, almost everything) to enhance your knowledge about relationships with men. Are you ready? Good, then let's begin.

During an age in which increasing numbers of top-choice men appear to be opting for serial dating and view monogamy as a dirty word, it is critical to have a ring formula for dating these men towards marriage. With the premium for good men at an all-time high, you simply cannot afford to date without a ring formula – a formula for getting married. What's your ring formula?

For a man to marry you, you must be able to meet his every need in ways that exceed even his highest expectations. He must view you as a sparkling diamond, a one-of-a-kind woman whom he must marry to keep all to himself. In order to get that ring on your finger, you must first embody the beauty, class, and glow of the highest quality diamond from within. You must know the needs and wants of your man inside and out and be able to meet them at his beck and call.

But what happens when your man doesn't communicate his needs? What happens when your man appears content to date you indefinitely but never propose? What happens when you feel like you're on a soul train carousel of Mr. Wrongs or faced with the idea of having to share your Mr. Right with half of the city? What do you do when you are the sparkling diamond, but your mate is a cubic zirconium? It's time to create THE RING FORMULA, a foolproof plan that takes your MR. RIGHT off the market and gets that ring on your finger.

Some women work from sun up to sun down preparing their bodies to lure the perfect man. In the end, however, they are surprised when superficial beauty alone fails to secure the prize. What they fail to develop is a superior game plan or formula that effectively eliminates the competition and wins them the matrimonial prize of Mr. Right.

Tens of thousands of amazingly beautiful, highly intelligent, and phenomenally talented women surprisingly have forgotten their inherent diamond status and the power that sharing that inner beauty holds in luring good men. I was surprised to find that many women didn't know the first thing about what men really wanted in a wife and too often relied on superficial qualities and sex to attract a husband. Being true to my profession as a psychologist, I decided to inquire to analyze the antecedent to this problem.

I was shocked to learn how little modern-day women knew about the true needs of men. First, most women were honest when they responded that they were completely confused about what men wanted and were eager to take notes and get the answers quickly. A second group of women never even thought about men's needs and felt that the courting process was all about them. They were oblivious to the idea that men like to be courted and taken care of as well. The third group gave some of the most ridiculous answers I've ever heard, and I knew it was time to help.

I heard answers ranging from great mind-blowing sex, all the food they could eat, beer, a remote control, video models, "yes" women, and on and on, ad nauseam. Ok, I'm being a little facetious, but I couldn't help but grow concerned because I had no idea that women were so clueless. It's amazing how different the thought process between men and women can be without good, healthy dialogue. I quickly began to see the true problem. While women have spent years of their lives in advanced study for their occupations, they apparently skipped the freshman course on how to court a man.

One group of women knew exactly how to attract and court good, eligible men. For the most part, these happily married women had taken lessons from the older generation on what men want and exactly how to give it to them. They put their knowledge to use and frequently relied on their fathers, mothers, aunts and sisters as consultants to keep their men coming back for more.

The conversations I had with these women made me want to marry them on the spot because they clearly knew something that so many single women did not—how to speak the language of men. Their every word and story about how they took care of their men was like playing the extended version of my favorite song over and over again. There was even a stark difference in how they treated me as we conversed about relationships. It got to the point where I could tell within the first five minutes, before any words about the book were discussed, who clearly knew versus who was clueless.

The more women I spoke with, the more it became clear that knowledge truly is power. For the first time, I began to empathize and understand these women's dilemma. They wanted to please and satisfy their men, but had never been taught techniques on courtship. In fact, many argued about the necessity of courting men at all.

Since these women were never properly taught, they were left to date without a training manual to guide their quest for love. They were like an archer with no bow. They clearly saw the target but lacked the proper tools to hit the mark. Adding to the dilemma is the fact that men certainly won't tell you what you're doing wrong during the process. They want to avoid conflict, and they expect you to know already.

For these reasons, single women have been forced to use what they have—*a woman's perspective*—but have failed miserably. The byproduct, unfortunately, has been a combination of loneliness, a series of painfully disappointing relationships, and eventual anger towards men. At its worst, this anger, based on a history of negative experiences with men, has resulted in low expectations and a subsequent self-fulfilling prophecy of unhappy relationships. Out of these bad experiences come some of the following wrongheaded overgeneralizations:

"All men are the same; they only want sex and can't appreciate a good woman with morals."

"Most men are intimidated by women who are better educated than they are."

"Men are intimidated by women who have their own car, house, and finances."

After listening to hundreds of baseless theories, and hearing horror stories about dating, I decided to ask one question: "Who taught you how to court men?" Their answers were telling. Many women revealed that they were self-taught, received instructions from their single girlfriends or, worst of all, learned from no one at all.

It was clear that something needed to happen. The time was right to create a crash course for all the beautiful but misinformed women in the world. Who better to learn from about what men truly want in a wife than a man ... who is also a psychologist?

Over the past fifteen years, I have dated, or been in serious relationships with two attorneys, one television network President, an *American Idol* contestant, Miss Black Georgia, two physicians, one health educator, one realtor, one nurse/model, three educators, one mechanical engineer, three psychologists, one flight attendant and one fashion designer.

They were all phenomenal women, and I was not intimidated by any of them. In fact, it was their intelligence, confidence and strength that attracted me to them. These relationships ended because of career moves, loss of chemistry/friendship, or personal immaturity. In many cases, the relationship had simply run its course.

Many of these women knew exactly what I wanted and, as a result, I was fiercely loyal, thankful and loving. On the other hand, some of the other potentially promising relationships never even got off the ground. They made huge mistakes that, unfortunately, had the opposite effect than expected, and I lost interest.

Being a "typical" man, I neglected to tell them what they were doing wrong during the courtship. Why? I wanted to avoid conflict, and I didn't feel I needed to. As a woman, should you tell a man how to kiss you, or would you expect him to know already? Having to give instructions about everything takes all the intrigue and excitement out of the relationship.

Early on, there were times when I was tempted to tell dates that they were making huge mistakes, but I remained silent. All of a sudden, after what appeared to be a perfect date or evening, I simply stopped calling. Don't you just hate me?

I would eventually call out of courtesy, and I could feel the confusion, pain and anguish emanating from the other end of the line. I could feel the question, "What did I do wrong?" seeping through the phone, but due to pride, they never asked. With some, the conversation would be brief, but I would talk with others, as friends, for hours. The funny thing is that once they got to know me and learned the secrets of my needs, we dated again until one of the above reasons occurred and ended the relationship.

I make no apologies for writing this book to make my life and every other man's life easier. Men prefer relationships without a lot of drama, miscommunication and arguing so I am using this book to give women a head start in understanding us. I am convinced that women who understand men have significantly more power and happiness in relationships.

Knowledge truly is power and is critical to successfully courting a man. It's no secret that men are not the best communicators, especially when it comes to expressing our needs to women. Many of us simply were not raised that way. Unlike women, rarely will you find men engaged in hours of conversation with one another arguing about what they need in order to settle down or get married. The reason is that we already know and agree with one another. We all want the same thing—a woman who understands us and knows how to take care of us just like mama.

This book will provide you with unlimited access to the psyche of the enigmatic male. I'm going to tell you exactly what men want and how to give it to us. This book is your study guide, so take notes, and use them in your next relationship. This book will even provide you with the exact language for wooing and loving your man. You and your MR. RIGHT can thank me later.

As a psychologist, I will admit that some men have serious issues that complicate the dating process; however, in the famous words of GI Joe, "Knowing is half the battle." I promise to take good care of you. And in doing so, I will give you the secrets of how to take care of the mind, body and soul of a man.

I'll teach you (1) how to flirt to attract marriage minded men (2) how to distinguish Mr. Right from Mr. I-say-all-the-right-things, (3) how to get inside your man's head, so you no longer have to guess incorrectly about what he's thinking, (4) how to get over insecurities (5) how to express your feelings and opinions without running him away, (6) how to make him want to commit (that's right, I did say *commit*), (7) how to get him to notice you and only you, and (8) how to deal with his meddlesome and/or dysfunctional family. So sit back, forget everything you think you thought you knew, and get your popcorn ready as you learn the secrets behind what men really want in a wife.

Honestly, I'm excited about the competitive advantage that any woman who reads this book will have over the woman who does not. As a motivational speaker, I have found the formula for success involves asking the company what information it would like covered, writing a speech that covers those very same points, and cashing that check as I am applauded for what I was told to say! It's like having honey in the bank, and yes, I did say *honey*.

Learning the secrets of what men desire from the women they choose to marry before you enter into a relationship will yield similarly sweet results for you. You'll be paid with what you really want—your very own MR. RIGHT who just happens to be holding the most spectacular diamond ring you've ever seen. And, yes, it will be perfectly sized for your finger.

Now, get your honeymoon destinations and your wedding fingers ready as I reveal the ring formula for dating towards marriage.

Formula ONE

LEARN HOW TO COOK: NURTURE A MAN'S SOUL

"There is more to dating than just looking cute." Your grandmother told you that the key to a man's heart is through his what? His *what*? His stomach! But did you listen? Some of you did and some of you didn't. I can hear the women's liberation movement ready to march now, but read on. I promise you will change your mind shortly. After you read this chapter, you must decide whether you would rather be Julia or Dr. Angela.

Dr. Angela was a petite, yet well-proportioned physician with velvety, evenly toned skin that was magazine-cover perfect. She had dark, piercing eyes and full, inviting lips. She had a mean shoe game and delighted in being fashionably accessorized and professionally manicured and pedicured. She had a cutting-edge hairstyle that was always freshly cropped. Her perfume of choice, Escada Magnetism, was used in just the right amount to linger faintly after she had passed by. Needless to say, Dr. Angela was well versed in the art of creating a desirable female image.

On a particular evening out on the town, she was keeping it simple—wearing a red silk well-fitted blouse that revealed just enough to tease but not enough to show everything she was working with, matching red boots that were just high enough to tempt but that distinguished her from a "professional shoe model," and black fitted designer stretch jeans. In her style of dress, men would smile coyly as she approached, and yell "DAAAYYYM" as she walked past.

Angela had a charmingly appealing personality. She had a comfortable knack for attracting men and was an absolute professional when it came to flirting. It was plain to see that she was confident in using her feminine wiles as evidenced by her first interaction with Jeff.

Angela met Jeff at a fashionably upscale happy hour spot in trendy downtown Atlanta that had a reputation for bringing out quality, eligible men who were all about their business. These men were known for having their own houses, one or two luxury cars, and sufficient bank accounts to handle buying a woman a drink or two and much more. Women knew to strike quickly and hard because the cream of the crop frequented The Martini Club to get their mix of good times and good men.

Being a native of Atlanta, Angela knew all the right spots and when to arrive. Since she was also socially perceptive, she arrived before the trendy crowd and competition. Angela was on a mission to get a man or at least a quality date. She was definitely not there to party, preferring to entertain her MR. RIGHT at home.

As she surveyed the field, she spotted Jeff, a six-feet-three Adonis who physically portrayed everything she was looking for. Muscular and lean with handsomely chiseled features, he was positioned at the bar dressed in a dark, navy business suit, spit-polished shoes that reflected his take-charge persona, and brushed twenty-four-karat-gold cufflinks engraved with his initials, JAK.

It was obvious that he took extreme care in his grooming, even down to the warm aroma of his aftershave lotion. What really captured Angela's attention, though, was that he was holding a snifter of Chivas Regal 25 with a pair of the largest hands she had ever seen.

Angela tingled with excitement, wanting to know more. Her initial approach was subtle, complimenting him on his cufflinks and coquettishly inquiring if "JAK" was someone who was successful at what he did. He laughed approvingly, introduced himself as Jeff, and easily carried the conversation. Quite naturally, she laughed at all of his jokes and made sure to touch his arms and chest when making a point, apologizing each time to make sure she had not stepped outside the boundaries of politeness.

"I'm sorry, JAK," she teased. "Is it OK if I touch you when I speak? I have a bad habit of doing that, so please ignore it if it gets on your nerves." She gave him a wink as she sought his approval.

She consulted her newly found love interest on what drink to order, hesitated when he offered to buy her another, and acquiesced when he made a strong point. Throughout the evening's conversation, she never mentioned that she was a doctor, instead focusing on her personal interests and places she liked to go.

Angela left The Martini Club around eight PM, but not with Jeff. Being a seasoned dater, she knew better and wanted him to take pursuit. She had taken the initial steps in showing she was interested. Now she would wait on his response. She did leave, however, with confirmed dinner reservations for the following night. Angela considered the night a success. She had her man, did not have to compete to get him, did not "waste" her outfit, and was in the bed watching *Girlfriends* by eleven o'clock. It was the perfect night.

Angela and Jeff dated for three months. During that time, they ate out most of the time, went to the park, and saw movies. They spoke on the phone almost every night, and she was impressed that Jeff was an excellent listener and very attentive. She really liked him but did not become clingy or demanding. She avoided discussing sex overtly, but she let him know that she would consider it "with the right guy." She laughed honestly at his jokes, did not interrupt his conversation, and listened when he was upset. When she felt the relationship was solid, she allowed herself to be intimate with him. She was affectionate enough to arouse his curiosity and make him desire more.

However, somewhere between euphoria and ecstasy, something went wrong. Instead of Jeff's calling more and showing more affection, he called less and became distant. He was no longer available on both Friday and Saturday nights and, eventually, was unavailable on both nights. His calls felt more like check-ins than a genuine, sincere desire to converse and spend time with her. Angela was flabbergasted. When he suddenly stopped calling altogether, she was literally in shock. She waited an entire two weeks, giving him every possible excuse in the book while rationalizing the sudden change in attention: Perhaps he became extra busy at work, or went out of town and forgot to call, or worse yet, suffered a death in the family.

Before long, Angela realized her worst fear. Jeff had met somebody new. He admitted it, and even had the nerve to tell her "it was serious." She thought, "And we weren't? Was I just a plaything for you to bounce around until you found something *serious*?"

Her insides boiled like lava, but she maintained her cool because her pride was bigger than her anger. She listened intently to his explanation with her phone couched between her ear and shoulder as she fiercely destroyed stress ball after stress ball with her fingernails. She began to light a small fire in her mind with Jeff in the middle. He went on and on for what seemed liked hours about *this wonderful connection* he had with this other woman—Julia.

Without ever having met her, Angela instinctively hated Julia, but she played the supportive friend role. "I'm disappointed, but I want you to be happy, Jeff," feigned Angela. Emotionally destroyed and psychologically undone, Angela vacillated between dating women, becoming a nun, or settling for the guy at work who had been after her for weeks, despite the fact that he had no attractive qualities whatsoever.

"What does this chick have that I don't?" she wondered. "Did she give it up faster? Is she prettier, have a larger ass, slimmer waist, freakier, bisexual? What?" Angela was unable to come to a clear rationalization, and all of her theories were wrong.

When she finally met Julia, she thought Jeff had lost his mind. Angela evaluated herself as being better educated and prettier. She had a better body and a much better shoe game. In short, she was more woman than Julia was. When Jeff introduced her to Julia, she played the supportive friend role that matched the way Jeff introduced her (A--hole), but inside she was devastated and confused.

She had imagined Julia to be a goddess who looked like Beyoncé, but Julia wasn't even the equivalent to a background singer for Destiny's Child. Angela's ego needed Julia to be clearly superior to her, so she could make sense of it all. For the first time in her life, Angela was without all the right answers.

In reality, it had very little to do with any of her theories, phobias or ego-laden lies. Julia knew one thing that Angela did not. Julia knew how to cook.

Julia was from the country—Vicksburg, Mississippi to be exact. Her grandmother and mother taught her how to cook, and she had been cooking for her father and brothers for years. Julia even grew tomatoes in the backyard and shopped at Whole Foods or the Farmers Market every week. Every fruit and vegetable in her house was fresh, healthy, and delectable.

Julia was a schoolteacher and an aspiring author. She did not have the flashy wardrobe like Angela, yet she was fashionable. She manicured her own nails from time to time and owned a few pairs of moderately priced heels. She rarely went to happy hours or to the club unless she was invited to someone's birthday party. She wanted to wait until marriage to have sex, but admitted that she had slipped up a couple of times well into long-term relationships. Jeff respected her celibacy and did not pressure her.

Given Jeff's lifestyle with Angela, you may be wondering where he and Julia met. It was at the grocery store. In fact, they met when he was on the way to Angela's house, picking up a frozen pizza for dinner. As he stood behind Julia in the checkout line, Jeff noticed the okra, whole corn, pork tenderloin, bell peppers and fresh collard greens that Julia had in her basket. He asked if she was planning a big celebration. She answered, "No, I like to cook a lot, and I'm making dinner for the men at my job because we all have to work late grading papers for final exams this week."

Ladies, let me tell you, it was love at first sight! Angela and that frozen pizza didn't stand a chance. Big Mama was right—the key to Jeff's heart was indeed through his stomach.

Before you chalk Jeff up be a man who just wanted a cook, you need to understand that there is unbelievable power in understanding the psychology of cooking for your man. There are three important phases when it comes to producing a meal: first, picking the healthiest, most succulent-looking ingredients; second, preparing the meal with the greatest of tender-loving care; and finally, presenting and savoring the mouth-watering combination of your efforts.

When a woman learns to cook, not just open a can and heat or microwave, she learns how to love and thus becomes a very powerful woman who is able to control even the strongest of men. Men grow attached to their moms because of the way she feeds and nurtures him through his formative years. Because of this, men are fiercely loyal to their mothers regardless of their flaws, shortcomings or prejudices, so if you plan to compete, you had better learn to fight fire with fire. Angela was fighting fire with ... well ... a strong shoe game. In the end, you can't eat shoes.

Is it any wonder that Julia was able to "steal" Jeff without even trying? In fact, she did not really steal him. Jeff came to her! The day they met, Julia was dressed in a jogging suit, tennis shoes and no makeup. Jeff saw Julia for what she truly was—a wholesome, clean-faced woman. Her willingness to nurture and feed Jeff's mind, body and soul was all that was required. One taste of Julia's good cooking and it was good-bye Angela. Angela? Angela who?

Julia's love was stronger than Angela's game. Angela scored favorably when it came to superficial appearances, but she was clearly outmatched when it came to pleasing and loving a man. While Angela was trying to lure Jeff with her feminine wiles, Julia was busy loving Jeff with her nurturing ways.

As it turned out, Julia was the one writing the dissertation on Jeff's needs. First, Julia had mastered the art of food selection. She knew how to pick savory fruits and vegetables. She preferred natural to processed, plump over scrawny, and healthy over sickly. She also knew that real men prefer the same thing in their women.

As Aretha sang, Julia was a "natural woman." She used natural products in her hair, ate only natural fruits and vegetables, kept her skin clear with natural products, exercised frequently, and maintained regular visits to the doctor. She didn't drink, except on special occasions, and never smoked a day in her life. Although Jeff smoked when he was with Angela, Julia's healthful approach to life immediately caused Jeff to lose his taste for nicotine and quit smoking.

Julia knew that men like natural beauty because they have a fear that women they meet on Friday night will not look the same Saturday morning. Men secretly fear that women who do not take great care of themselves, neglect regular exercise, and do not eat right may get fat, unattractive and ill in their older age.

Men understand the aging process and want a woman who ages gracefully and still looks great at forty, fifty, and sixty years old. Men don't ever want to think of a day when they are no longer sexually attracted to their spouses. By taking care of herself, Julia immediately made herself a competitor to Angela who, by contrast, would rather eat out than cook any day. Why put the strain on her nails with so many great restaurants in Atlanta?

Julia also knew the true definition of soul food. She understood that soul food was more spiritual in nature, whether it was black-eyed peas, collard greens or sweet potatoes. Soul food is literally food to nourish the soul. When cooking for Jeff, she picked healthy ingredients that he said he liked or referred to in conversations with her. She thought of him when she shopped and added in special spices depending on her mood and growing feelings toward Jeff. She put her soul into cooking and fed it to Jeff, and Jeff noticed. Boy did Jeff notice!

In exchange for the nurturing love Julia gave, Jeff reciprocated in many beautifully simple ways. When she arrived at home with the groceries, she didn't even have to honk. He would meet her at her house (some twenty minutes away from his) if he knew she had been shopping, just to unload the car. Before long, he even enjoyed shopping with her and discussing the meals for the week.

Julia's car never collected a trace of dirt without Jeff washing and waxing it to perfection. There was not one loose screw he didn't tighten. He even loaded virus protection software on her computers at home and work. Jeff wanted to take care of Julia to reciprocate the obvious care and nurturance she was giving him.

Before long, Jeff was in the kitchen all the time. While Julia was cooking, he was reading aloud the newest article in *Essence* magazine, or improving something in the kitchen: fixing the garbage disposal, assembling a towel rack, building a lazy Susan, or surprising her with new cutting boards from

Crate & Barrel.

Before long, they were cooking side-by-side because he thoroughly enjoyed her company and her spirit. He had even more fun stirring, tasting, and putting things on slow cook while she kissed him passionately while dressed in way-too-short shorts, his basketball jersey, and the new red heels he bought her.

Jeff and Julia cooked all the time, and sometimes the meals just simmered while they enjoyed each other. When they did finally eat, their conversation was magnificent. They would talk for hours and hours over Julia's peach cobbler, the occasional dessert wine, and the natural wood fire Jeff lit especially for the occasion.

Each meal was a special occasion for them. He listened to her every desire, and vowed to support her in any way he could. She listened to his goals and ambitions, and never hesitated to fix something special for his big meetings. It was not long before Jeff built up a psychological, physical and emotional dependence on Julia and her soul cooking.

Six months into the relationship, Julia weakened and had sex with Jeff, and Jeff made sure to feed her with all his soul. He also said that he would respect her wishes and wait until marriage to be with her again. Marriage; this was sweet music to Julia's ears, her mother's ears, and her grandmother's ears, and Julia decided to weaken just one more time ... to celebrate with the man who was to become her husband.

Poor Angela. She had brought a pocketknife to a gunfight! While she had flirtatiously desired to know if JAK was "good at what he did," in the end, Jeff was more interested in being taken care of himself. Needless to say, Angela did not attend the wedding and, a year later, did everything in her power to avoid crying when she saw Julia's stomach protruding with twins.

Take a moment to think back to the decision required

before you read the next chapter. Would you rather be Dr. Angela or Julia? If you still want to be Angela, keep reading. I hope that you will find yourself somewhere between these pages and make the decision to do what it really takes to date towards long-term commitment and marriage. If you decide you want to be Julia, keep reading. Most definitely, you will learn more formulas for getting closer to that ring; whichever your desire, just keep on reading.

Application Section

Okay, I realize that you may be thinking, "If I really have to cook to get and keep a good man...I'm in trouble!" If so, relax because there are certainly relationships that work out where couples rotate cooking or the man is the primary or only chef in the house. What is most important is developing the proper **mindset** about nurturing your man.

If you walk around feeling like you are giving too much or changing who you are by cooking then you are selling yourself short as a nurturer. Additionally, you have very little chance of attracting and keeping MR. RIGHT. Why? Simple, men equate nurturing with love. So, if you don't nurture, then you have no worth to a man because you cannot love. Remember, this is the process by which moms bond to their sons and that bond lasts for a lifetime. In man- language, a woman who does not nurture is not a woman and definitely cannot be his wife.

Adopting the willing mindset and practice of nurturing your man is an absolute necessity if you want him to see you as marriage material. If you are still not quite there yet then I challenge you to candidly and honestly answer the following questions before you miss out on successfully dating the man of a lifetime who, by the way, could be just one, carefully prepared meal away.

1) Would/Will you cook for your son or daughter? Why or why not?

absolutely; I would want my child to have well balanced meals.

2) What emotions come to mind when you think about eating your mother's cooking?

warm, feeling loved, eating good food! at home.

(Based on previous questions) Is it possible that men have the same needs and desires in regards to feeling nurtured that children do? The answer is YES. In fact, they require it because their mothers trained them to look for those qualities in a wife.

3) Do you desire to be the primary source (outside of God) for nurturing and loving your man?

absolutely

4) Are you truly willing to give up the daily power of nurturing and nourishing your man and future children simply because you dislike or are not yet an excellent cook?

no; I cook!

5) Would you prefer your future grand-children to have a mother who cooks over one who does not (all things being equal)?

no, I want my daughter or daughter-in-law to cook.

6) Do you want control, credit, and direct responsibility for making your man and family healthy?

I do!

7) Are you sure you want to bypass the daily opportunity to reassure, reaffirm and demonstrate that you love, care and actively nurture your man and family?

I do not want to

by pass that opportunity

See, now I have you thinking differently. Courting a man toward marriage requires more than just looking cute and being his little sex kitten. In fact, these qualities don't hold a marriage together.

When a man contemplates marriage he rarely thinks about divorce. He expects and believes that the relationship will last forever. Therefore, a man dates to find out just how great of a long-term nurturer you are. This allows the man to be able to see you as a great lover, future mother, best friend and wife.

Let's be practical about this. Have you noticed that most wives cook for their husbands and children? Do you really think they started doing that *after* they got married? How in the world did her husband know beyond a shadow of doubt that she was a great nurturer before he decided to marry her?

After all, what made him, in his right mind; decide to stop dating the plethora of women on the market to settle down with one...forever? Simple, she upgraded him daily by taking care of his every need so he had no desire for another woman. Additionally, he experienced being taken care of better than he ever had before (next to mama) in his entire dating life. A man's selfish nature then kicks in and he produces what is required to maintain that level of nurturance for life... the diamond wedding ring you deserve for all your hard work. After all, diamonds are forever and men will FOREVER be hungry.

In summary, date a man like his wife NOW and EXPECT him to produce a ring to keep you forever. Besides, conditioning a man to be dependent upon you for daily nourishment and nurturing will leave you in control for the rest of the relationship. Remember ladies, dating is just a showcase for how awesome his life could be with you as his wife. Give him all the tender love and care you can muster and watch him behave accordingly.

Don't panic if the ring is slow to arrive. Just keep cooking, ego-stroking and loving him until he comes around. The key is to EXPECT a ring in return and not to be afraid to leave if he fails to do so. Exercising the power of taking all that lemon-peppered shrimp, chocolate cake, physical affection, love and ego-stroking to another more appreciative man is empowering. It's also a very necessary step towards bringing your man to his knees, where by the way, he should be to propose.

I'm getting excited even while writing this. When you date a *deserving* man as if you are already his wife and then leave him because he failed to make your relationship official, you hold the upper hand while also creating a drug effect. That's right, withdrawal.

The loss of love he suffers when you leave causes withdrawal symptoms that make him break down and come back for a permanent fix! A woman who is convinced of her beauty (inner and outer) should never be afraid to take her show on the road for a wiser man who will show her the love and appreciation that she deserves.

Smile when he says he's "afraid" or "not ready" after two years and prepare to pack your bags but keep them light. He'll come running to find you soon enough, that is if you haven't moved on to a more deserving man who knows a wife when he sees one! Go figure, a male psychologist is giving women the power and psychological control in relationships! I feel like a traitor. Well, not really because I can't imagine too many men complaining when their stomachs and egos are no longer growling for attention. After all, how much processed and fast food can a man eat and not die an early death?

Wow, what time is it? Almost six o'clock, dinner time. Ladies, you had better pull out those cookbooks, backrubs and compliments about his intelligence quick, fast and in a hurry! I see a million emotionally-starved men who are looking for a Ring Formula Woman to feed and satisfy their mind, bodies and soul. Can you say, "Hunny, soup's on!"

Formula TWO

GET THE GORILLAS OUT OF YOUR HOUSE AND GET RID OF INSECURITY

"How can you expect a man to be confident in loving you if you don't fully love yourself?" Gorillas are those massively hairy obstructions in our lives that we know exist because they take up lots of space and stink to the top of the rafters, yet we flagrantly ignore them, hoping that anyone who enters our life will also be oblivious. Gorillas take a long time to grow to their obtrusive size, and while they might have been cute when they were little, once full-grown, they are not only unattractive; they are downright dangerous in the development of a relationship.

A man is most attracted to a woman who is confident in her abilities, happy with herself, and emotionally secure. Therefore, when it comes to relationships, ladies, leave your gorillas at the zoo. There are three of these gorillas: insecurity, lack of trust and selfishness. Any of these can, and likely will, destroy your relationships. In this age, where eligible bachelorettes outnumber bachelors by staggering numbers, you simply cannot allow gorillas to reside unchecked in your house.

There are already too many men who are unavailable, against monogamy, and/or have significant baggage themselves for you to run off quality men with your gorillas.

Yes, negative relationships from the past can affect your ability to trust and feel secure, but you will need to heal quickly or choose to sit on the sidelines until you are ready to get back in the game. The good men on the playing field have many options these days. You cannot afford to ignore or wait to address your issues and still expect to be a member of the A-team.

When it comes to establishing the relationship you have always wanted, you must be ready to present your best package. In this chapter, you will meet two very different women. It is up to you to decide if you want to be like Sabrina or Alena.

Sabrina was a spectacularly built, petite sister with flawless skin. Her striking brown eyes screamed trouble, but her smile was too inviting to pass up. Her auburn hair draped her back, and her accessories drew attention to her especially busty frame (for someone five-feet-five). She preferred bright-colored mid-cut dresses that displayed her sleek neckline, rocked a perfect French manicure, and always wore four-inch heels. If it were not for working out, she would not even own a pair of tennis shoes.

With curves that put a Coke bottle to shame, it was no wonder that Sabrina made a healthy living cheerleading, modeling and appearing in commercials. She was even asked to pose in *Playboy*, but she respectfully refused. She liked the attention and the limelight but had no plans of being objectified.

Sabrina had recently moved to the Battle Creek, Michigan area from Atlanta to finish an advanced degree. While focused on her studies, she longed for the Atlanta nightlife and found the quality of available men slim in conservative Battle Creek. Born with the ability to turn heads, she had no problem getting attention, but it was from the wrong age group. At twenty-seven, she found most of the quality men her age to be already married or single for obvious reasons. The older men, even worse, would proposition her for an affair or were so grotesquely out of shape that it was sickening.

Her friends back in Atlanta kept pressuring her to get a profile on the Internet as they bragged about meeting quality men online. Since she was out of viable options in Battle Creek, Sabrina decided she had nothing to lose. Within a couple of weeks of posting her profile on a popular dating site, Sabrina struck gold.

Sabrina got lucky when she met Rico. His was the first profile that she explored. Despite being skeptical of finding love online, she was intrigued with this brother. Rico flashed a smile that was as wide as the Texas landscape with enough electricity to light up Las Vegas. His profile bragged that he had a 6'0 athletic build, and he held a graduate degree in sociology. He was single, twenty-eight, had no kids, and had an obvious eye for beautiful women, evidenced by his friends' links.

She wondered how in the world he could be on the market. Is he a player, too full of himself, or gay/bisexual? After all, he did reside in Atlanta—the black, gay capital of the world. She delved into his profile and failed to find any evidence to eliminate him. In fact, he was a God-fearing brother who openly desired marriage and children and listed mentoring and sports as hobbies. Having little confidence in online dating, she reluctantly sent him a friend request, and he answered immediately. He was online and could see the pictures she had playfully uploaded. He was smitten and assertively began flirting, making known his desire to do more than eyeball her photos. Rico said he wanted the real deal.

After just a few days of online flirting, Sabrina was exchanging emails with Rico from work, text messaging, and spending late evenings lying in her bed talking to her newly found Romeo. The phone conversations would eventually get steamy as he talked about his desire for long vacations in intimate, picturesque locations overlooking expansive beaches.

The moments of cozy silence that nestled between spicy

dialogues gave clues that their imaginations were cosmically in tune. Sabrina was falling for Rico in a big way, but there was one major problem. Despite the sensuous hours of romantic interlude, she had never seen this man! How could she be sure that the pictures she had downloaded to a personal file were his real photos? After all, those could have been pictures of his brother. Sabrina was determined to find out.

Two months into the relationship, Sabrina started spending time on Travelocity looking for inexpensive airfare to Atlanta. She was ready to get married and would just as well not waste her time on someone who wasn't all he said he was.

She didn't book the ticket immediately, but she knew that this would be her next step. Intuition turned to reality when she arrived back at her condominium around 6:00 PM and checked the mail. She sifted through bill after bill, junk mail and advertisements until she came to the very last piece. In her hand, she held an ornately decorated envelope that screamed "wedding invitation." She squealed aloud as she discovered that her friend, Samantha, was marrying her high school sweetheart next month ... in Atlanta.

Samantha was one of the cheerleaders from Sabrina's squad. Sabrina was ecstatic but confused about why she was getting such late notice. She pulled out her new Blackberry Storm phone and called to congratulate and bless Samantha out. Before the call could connect, the incoming call light blinked. It was Samantha, asking Sabrina why she hadn't RSVP'd yet. Apparently, there had been a significant delay in forwarding the mail to her new address in Michigan. After they cleared the air, Sabrina and Samantha laughed and talked for what seemed like hours. Finally, Samantha dropped a surprise on Sabrina. Not only did she want Sabrina to come to the wedding, but she also wanted her to sing with a full band behind her. Sabrina gladly accepted and went to bed with a wide smile on her face.

Around midnight she woke up and realized that this was her opportunity to see if Rico was the real deal. She called him and gave him the good news. She wondered if he would now fake moves and expose himself as a fraud. To her delight, however, he was equally excited and even indicated that he was looking forward to seeing her too. He announced, "Now I get to see firsthand what all the hype is about." Excited and aroused, Sabrina couldn't sleep for hours, thinking about the wedding, choice of songs, and meeting Rico. She could not help but wonder if the two events were cosmically connected.

Sabrina arrived in Atlanta with a freshly styled wedding hairdo, newly manicured nails and toes, and a flattering bright yellow and brown chiffon dress that would have Rico and every other man in Atlanta salivating. She also packed her black sequined formal to match the live band's attire for her performance. Sabrina had everything she needed to sing and go out on the town with Rico.

Sabrina had an absolute ball at the wedding. The liquor was flowing, all her girls attended, and the catering was fit for Roman royalty. Samantha looked radiant in her ivory wedding gown embroidered with encrusted pearls from her waist to the edge of her cathedral length train. Samantha's soon-to-be-married glow served as inspiration for Sabrina to sing her heart out. Sabrina tore down the house with her renditions of the unforgettable love songs "So Beautiful" and "So Amazing." Not a dry eye was left in the ballroom by the time Samantha kissed Matthew to seal their heavenly matrimony. The electricity in the room was potent, and Sabrina found herself feverishly excited about starting her own wedding story with Rico afterward.

Rico arrived in the lobby of the Ritz Carlton Hotel around 8:30 PM dressed in all black. From his tailored shirt and cashmere dress coat all the way down to his Stacy Adams, Rico's persona oozed of intrigue, confidence and mystery. As he admired the architectural splendor of the five-star hotel, with its twenty-foot ceilings, marbled flooring, regal red oriental rugs, and cherry wood paneling, he was distracted by the far more beautiful scene of cleavage, long legs and fragranced women who filed out of the wedding reception. Sabrina was running late, but this was one time Rico certainly didn't mind.

Suddenly he noticed the familiar face of an old friend in the crowd, as well as the gorgeous woman who accompanied her. "Rico, darling, this is my friend Tessa. What are you doing in the lobby of the Ritz Carlton? Got a hot date with one of my home-girls?"

Kalicia was the younger sister of his brother's ex-girlfriend. They exchanged hugs, and he extended a courteous greeting to Kalicia's friend. Rico figured that Kalicia and Sabrina knew one another.

Within the next minute, Sabrina made her grand entrance after having changed into a dazzling ensemble that made Rico's eyes fill with lust. Kalicia and her friend complimented Sabrina, brushing her down and "mmm hmming" from head to toe. While Rico was busy gawking, Kalicia gave Sabrina the thumbs up. She jokingly informed Rico that she had already given Sabrina the scoop on him and that she would be expecting her check, wedding invitation and naming rights to their first-born child.

Sabrina hugged Kalicia, strangely ignored Tessa, and gave Rico an introductory peck on the cheek. Rico found the interaction among the three to be odd but was too consumed with Sabrina's almond-colored thighs and six-inch heels to make much of it at the time.

Sabrina was everything she said she was. She was superstar gorgeous and sexy with a smile to warm up Alaska. She was extremely busty to be so petite, but Rico was not complaining. He had hoped that Sabrina would look as good in person as in her pictures, but he got even more than imagined.

Pictures certainly didn't do Sabrina justice compared to her persona and aura in the flesh. Calm, smooth and possessing a roaming eye when he arrived, Rico was eager, alert and keenly focused on Sabrina's every move now.

The feeling was obviously mutual as Rico caught Sabrina shooting a look to Kalicia that signaled he wasn't the only one who was pleasantly surprised. They bid farewell to Kalicia and company and walked toward Rico's black Escalade. After politely ushering Sabrina into the SUV, Rico verbalized his sentiments. "Wow, you look nice!" Rico was at a loss for words.

Sabrina's response was cordial, but the look in her eye failed to exude appreciation. It was an ominous sign of things to come over the next few hours. Rico brushed it off and confidently sped away to their destination.

Sabrina was always cracking jokes on the phone, so he decided he would surprise her with tickets to the comedy club. On the way, Rico tried to make small talk in an attempt to jumpstart the chemistry they enjoyed over the phone and online. He inquired about her performance, the flight, and the overall wedding, but she met him with rather terse, cold one-word responses and little eye contact.

He inquired about the soul-train conga line, her family, and the overall mood for the evening. Still, Sabrina kept her answers short and void of substance. Assuming it was just nerves, Rico turned up the radio to lighten the mood and decided to give Sabrina a few minutes to get loose; however, the minutes began to pass slower and slower as Sabrina's funky attitude permeated every second of the commute.

"Sabrina, is everything OK?"

"Just peachy. No, actually, everything is just *nice*," was her frigid response.

Rico's facial expression made it clear that he was lost. "What do you mean by that?"

"You said that I just looked *nice* when you met me. Is that really what you think of me—that I'm ... *nice*?"

Rico sighed, cursing the Internet for not performing a personality assessment. He wanted to maintain an open mind and allow the evening to unfold. Sabrina was not having it. She demanded an answer. "Rico, is *nice* the best adjective a man of your intelligence could think of?"

Behold Gorilla #1: Insecurity!

"Not again," he thought, referring to his recent string of dates with gorgeous women with low self-images. Despite his intuition, Rico decided to gut it out; hoping his words and positive energy could carry the evening. "Sabrina, I didn't say you *just* looked nice. I said, "Wow, you look *Nice*! There is a stark difference, baby girl."

Sabrina continued her attack. "Rico, *nice* means *nice*, but don't worry about it; let's just pay and go in." Rico's instinct said, "Let's not," but before he knew it, he was in line.

With the long line, the chilly climate, and the iceberg reception from Sabrina, Rico didn't feel too confident about snuggling to stay warm or indulging in a pleasant conservation to distract him from the wintry mix of wind and thirty-one degree temperature.

He approached the bouncer and inquired about the wait and the fee to cut the line. The bouncer indicated, "Oh, about ten to fifteen minutes, or a dub" ($100), and motioned to the back of the line when Rico frowned, indicating that his dub was remaining in his wallet. Rico buttoned up his coat and reached for Sabrina's hand for good measure.

As they waited in cold silence, Sabrina could not help but notice all of the beautiful women in line. Secretly comparing herself to the other women, she wondered if Rico thought they looked better than she did. Which one was Rico most attracted to? Which one looks conniving and sneaky enough to try to push up on her date?

She gave a coy smile and asked him, "Rico, do you see any cuties in line? I know you like real thick Atlanta girls like the ones on your friends' profiles."

Rico shrugged, "I can't call it; I'm just ready to get inside." Irritated and needing a distraction from the cold and a harmonious conversation, he commented to the couple to his right, "It's cold as hell out here. I hope the comedian is funny. Who's the headliner tonight?"

Immediately, Sabrina grabbed his arm, pulled him over, and switched places with him, so she could serve as a buffer between Rico and the couple. She whispered to Rico, "These females are trifling. She needs to speak to her own man."

Behold Gorilla #2: Trust Issues

Rico was not getting a good feeling about Sabrina. She was playing all her cards, and he wondered if any of them were good. Suddenly, the bouncer allowed the frostbitten crowd to enter. The music, teriyaki chicken wings, and laughter shifted his attention and served as a shot of adrenaline for his mood.

He'd had a rough week and was convinced that no one, not even insecure Sabrina, was going to ruin it. His enhanced mood must have been contagious because Sabrina apologized and metamorphosed into the woman he had spent hours chatting with online. Like turning on a switch, she flashed a million-dollar smile and displayed that infectious personality that initially captured his attention. She burst into song with one of the sweetest, most melodious voices Rico had ever heard as she harmonized with the tunes of the DJ. She sang with passion and conviction. For a brief moment, Sabrina was back.

Rico enjoyed the surprise. Sabrina had flair, and he loved it. She even personalized the words of one of the songs. By the time the server seated them, Rico was beginning to ease back into the evening. While Sabrina was perusing the menu,

Rico was perusing Sabrina. He couldn't help but stare and marvel at her beauty.

Sabrina looked up and Rico smiled, not caring that he was busted. Then the green light switched to red. Sabrina got upset. She asked Rico to stop staring at her and began obsessing about the tiny moles on her face. "I hate these moles. I know you can barely see them, but they still bother me when people stare at them."

Remembering that she loved to crack jokes, Rico erupted in laughter because she had him going. His smile quickly dissipated when he realized that she was dead serious. He wondered if he was dating a beautiful cheerleader or Melman, the giraffe in the movie *Madagascar* who obsessed about his spots.

Sabrina began to bug out. She gave Rico a five-minute lecture on how he needed to look past her transgressions and how she was sick of everyone expecting her to look perfect all the time. Rico tried to get a word in. "I was admiring you. You look damn near perfect to me."

Stopping him in his tracks, she countered, "Damn near, Rico?"

"You know what I mean, Sabrina. This is getting ridiculous. Perhaps we should just not speak since you're so sensitive about *damn near* everything I say."

Sabrina was not about to let up. "Why don't you tell me what else you would like for me to change to please you? Go ahead and say it. You don't like cheerleaders because you think we're air-headed, or you would prefer for me to have thicker thighs and lips, or maybe I'm shaped too much like a little girl for you because I'm lacking the proverbial junk in the trunk you apparently can't live without."

Sabrina went on and on and on, conjuring up every possible flaw she could think of.

Rico tried to stop her. "Sabrina, would you please chill? All I want to do is have a good time and unwind with a beautiful woman. I have enough stress at work; I don't need to bring it to the comedy club. You can't be serious right now."

"Oh, I'm very serious, despite how air-headed you might think I am." She continued with her tirade becoming louder and louder as the show progressed. It was so bad that the comedian stopped the show because he thought Sabrina was going off on Rico.

He joked, "Damn. Who let Bobby and Whitney in the building? And it looks like Whitney is winning. Bobby, Bobby, you are the King of Pop, baby; stand up for yourself, dog. Nah, that's right, you're on parole. Don't say anything, man. Didn't you just get out last night? And why are you wearing all that black? Ladies and gentlemen, introducing Mr. Bobby Black, Bobby Zorro," and the jokes went on and on and on.

In trying to calm Sabrina, Rico had made himself a perfect target for the comedian. How embarrassing! After a rough week at work, he was looking forward to a wonderful night out on the town with Sabrina. Instead, it was turning into a nightmare.

Everyone knows not to respond and just laugh when a professional comedian clowns you, but not Sabrina. She was in a state of rage, and the fact that the comedian was male didn't help matters. She screamed back, "Why don't you lose some weight before you crack on people who actually are in shape?" Rico had a *Star Trek* moment and prayed that he could just teleport away.

The comedian obviously didn't watch *Star Trek* and was not amused. Rico tried to talk to Sabrina and explain that he was uncomfortable with public humiliation and would rather that she just chill. Sabrina refused to calm down.

"Nah, I'm not going to shut up and just bow down. If he's fat, he's just fat, and he knows it. And you should be able to handle a little criticism too since you have so much to say about me."

Behold Gorilla #3: Selfishness

The comedian, a national headliner, clowned Sabrina and Rico for the entire evening until they eventually had to leave. Sabrina never stopped arguing back and forth despite being on the losing end of the jokes. She didn't even care that Rico was being clowned, even though he hadn't said a word. He had to endure being called "a chump," "the missing member of the Backstreet Boys," and a "gay priest"! It got to the point where the comedian and audience were focusing more on Sabrina and Rico than on the actual show. Embarrassed, frustrated, and humiliated, Rico lit into Sabrina as soon as the door to the club closed behind them, finally silencing the mockery.

"You are crazy. You are one of the most beautiful women I have ever met, and you have managed to ruin every positive thought I had about you in less than an hour. You have issues you obviously needed to work out before you left the house. I'm going to take you back to the hotel and chalk this up as a date from hell."

"Well, call this the date from hell with the cheerleader who hates herself." Sabrina had finally said it. As the core of her anger spewed out, she began to cry, not uttering a word during the speedy ride back to the hotel.

Sabrina avoided eye contact with Rico, this time out of shame and embarrassment. When they arrived at the hotel, Rico didn't even offer to walk her upstairs. He was ready to go. Maybe he could salvage the evening and hit up a club or something. He needed to relax. He felt like a gorilla had accosted him without provocation.

To his surprise, Sabrina apologized, begged him not to leave, and invited him upstairs. Against his better judgment, or maybe thinking with the wrong head, he obliged. She apologized profusely and indicated that she had problems in the past with men because of her concerns about her body.

"No ... really?" Rico blurted out. He didn't feel the need to hold back as he also needed to vent. After moments of awkward silence, they settled in and began to watch a movie, *Gorillas in the Mist.* Since there was not much action on television or in the room, Rico decided to make it an early night.

"I'm going to call it a night, Sabrina, but it was real." He extended his arms to hug her and attempted to kiss her cheek.

The fireworks flared up once again. "You don't have to coddle me, Rico. I know you're only doing this out of obligation."

As he headed for the door, Sabrina pried one more answer out of her beleaguered date. "Hey, before you leave, could you answer a quick question for me?"

"Sure," he replied cautiously, keeping in mind how sensitive she had been to his earlier comments.

"You said that you didn't see half the things I see wrong with my body. I was just wondering what you meant because I need to know what to work on."

Rico shook his head, pulled his keys out his pocket, whispered "Start with your self-esteem," and left. As he was exiting the lobby doors, he ran into Kalicia and Tessa.

"How was it?" asked Kalicia nosily. Rico gave her a half-smile, shook his head and grumbled Sabrina or the three gorillas?"

The problem with Sabrina, which is a symptom of many insecure women, was that she forgot to leave her baggage at the door. It is a tragic mistake when insecurity, lack of trust and/or selfishness are/is allowed to mess up a promising relationship.

While this example may sound extreme, countless

Sabrinas allow their baggage to ruin the first, second or third date, thus cutting short the road to a long and promising relationship. The truth is that Sabrina should not have been dating in the first place. Instead of facing her gorillas privately, she chose to carry them out into the public eye.

A relationship is not the place to unleash your gorillas. The purpose of a relationship is to add value to each other's life. It is true that too many negative experiences can create a negative self-image. If you are at this point in life, take time to evaluate the good things in yourself. Reassure yourself that you have outstanding qualities, and work on believing that these qualities are real, admirable and qualify you as a person of worth.

Work hard to eliminate the cycle of despair and self-destruction that surfaces at the least inopportune times. Don't become overly critical and sensitive to the point that you harbor an image of beauty that no one can uphold.

Learn to become comfortable with your body image, blemishes and level of intellect, so you can project the beauty of your personality instead of the imperfection of your insecurities. The best way to achieve this is to overcome your self-absorption and focus on the needs of your partner. It doesn't happen overnight, but with time and practice, you will begin to see the beauty of life around you and the wonderfully unique role you play in it.

Despite popular opinion, men do realize that models and beauty queens go to great lengths to achieve a certain look. They know that women in these occupations spend an inordinate amount of time with personal trainers, makeup artists and hair stylists. In truth, most brothers don't prefer such high-maintenance women because it means there is too much emphasis on achieving the perfect image and too little time for them.

Men understand and appreciate that professional women simply don't have time to spend seven days a week in the gym or an hour a night taking milk baths. While men do expect women to look their best, most importantly they want their women to be REAL. Sabrina internalized all the hype about what women think men want—a perfect woman. In turn, she created a self-fulfilling prophecy of men rejecting her, though not for the reasons she stated. Insecurities are contagious. If you introduce them to your man, you will have a difficult time getting him to forget them.

So what should you do? Let's look at a different example. This time, I am letting you in on one of my own experiences in the field.

Alena was a 5'10" model-type with lightly tanned skin and naturally curly hair that hung down the middle of her back. Her full lips, curvy hips and supremely confident smile screamed, "Goddess with a Los Angeles zip code." Her form-fitting jeans, colorful and masterfully flattering tops, and high-heeled boots would cause horns to honk and brakes to pump simultaneously.

One night we were out at a local club having a good time at the bar. Alena indicated she was headed to the ladies' room while I remained seated, sipping on a drink. Within two minutes, Vicki, a 5'8" artsy type with a brick-house body, took the seat next to me. Before I could tell her it was taken, she began to impress me with her silver-tongued game and clever play on words. She was a spoken-word artist who certainly was not shy about displaying her unlimited repertoire of salacious poetry.

I was intrigued with her confidence and easy-going demeanor. We spoke for what seemed like fifteen minutes. I looked up to see where Alena was and was surprised to find her standing right behind me with the biggest smile on her face. I immediately stood up, introduced her to Vicki, and tried to explain. Surprisingly, Alena didn't need an explanation. She extended her hand, smiled at Vicki, genuinely complimented her on her ensemble, and invited her to join us at the bar since we were just hanging out. She even motioned for the couple adjacent to us to scoot down, so the three of us could sit together. I was amazed because I had never seen anything like that before.

Vicki was astute enough not to remain the third wheel for long. She thanked Alena for allowing her to keep me company while she was gone. As Alena sat down, Vicki complimented her on her outfit, shoes and taste in men. Alena laughed and joked, "Obviously, I can't let him out too much, so I think I'll just keep him to myself in the house from now on." We spent another five minutes conversing before Vicki decided to befriend another potential mate across the bar.

After Vicki left, I leaned over to Alena and inquired, "Why didn't you get mad? You didn't know whether I was trying to game her or not. I know it didn't look good."

Alena confidently smirked, "Alduan, that little girl can't touch all this," as she ran her manicured fingers down her body. She burst out laughing because, in reality, she was a very humble person.

"Seriously, Alduan, if you want to leave me for a lesser woman, it would be proof of very poor judgment on your part. You know what you have, so don't be silly," she confided as she motioned to the bartender to settle the tab. She pulled my hand, and we were off to the next spot for dessert and coffee.

With coolness and cunning, Alena's sex appeal quotient and position as "the only one" went up twelve notches that night. Vicki was cute, but after witnessing Alena's confidence, I would have been a fool to give Vicki a nod. I already had an absolute superstar on my arm. Interestingly, because Alena saw "no competition" with Vicki or any other women, neither did I. In fact, she could have left me at the bar all night, and I would not have gotten a single number because of how secure she was with herself.

Contrast this scenario to that of Sabrina and Rico. Sabrina

introduced the idea that she was not the "baddest" woman in the club. Rico thought she was, but Sabrina destroyed his image of her. By the end of the night, Rico was looking at other women because Sabrina had all but given him permission. She focused so much of her attention on other women that he felt obligated to look. In fact, he ended up befriending and dating Tessa, Kalicia's friend.

Through her petty jealousy, Sabrina had actually tipped him off about Tessa earlier. By not acknowledging her, Sabrina showed that she designated Tessa as a threat. Without having to bat an eyelash, Tessa impressed Rico with her beauty, class and self-confidence. After the roller-coaster ride with Sabrina and her three gorillas, he was ripe for the picking, and since he was already dressed for a night out, why waste his outfit?

Women, it's time to put the gorilla in its cage. A man loves a woman who loves herself first. You cannot expect men to love you if you don't first love yourself. You stand a much better chance of making a relationship work when you bring a healthy mind, body and soul into the mix. Thus, it is important to recognize your issues, do some soul searching and life exploration, and engage in counseling and prayer, so you can heal.

Past relationships that ended prematurely do hurt and damage self-esteem. Take time to heal and grow, and leave the baggage behind, so you don't ruin your next date with MR. RIGHT. In today's world, MR. RIGHTS are the valued prey. It's up to you to give the best of yourself, so you are guaranteed of getting and keeping your catch.

Application Section

Hopefully, by now you have decided to take a proactive stance towards addressing your own issues of insecurity, trust, and selfishness. The following exercises should help facilitate that process and help you to grow and heal to be ready for your next awesome relationship.

I purposely left a lot of room for you to write so fill up the entire space and if you need to, add more. Fact is, if you can't articulate what makes you unique and worthy of love to yourself, then how can you expect a man to fall in love with you? He can only see what you see, and if all he sees is insecurity then he is sure to get frustrated and seek a more secure partner.

1) Why should a man want to date you and only you for the rest of your life? What makes you uniquely special?

I am lovable, nurturing,
I do mostly what I
say I am going to do,
I love my friends and
family, I can cook, I

am clean, I am positive most of the time. I am loyal, fun, and purpose driver, I am willing to learn and I want a close, loving family. I want to know him emotionally, physically, spiritual, and increase him in any way necessary.

2) Think about a single man (even a male family member) that you know fairly well. In what ways could you add to his overall life? How could you improve his health, happiness, sense of hope, finances, overall fun, etc.? This exercise will help you to truly see the significant value that you add to a man.

I could balance him by cooking him better meals pay attention to what makes him happy such as his hobbies and gift him or treat him to the things he like, I can enjoy his hobbies with him.

3) List three major events that have adversely affected your self-confidence.

1) dating men who do not date mongomously

2) my father not being there giving me a sense of rejection - people walking away

3) me being indecisive about what I want to do in life.

The key to growing from pain versus allowing it to permanently debilitate you is to find the hidden meaning in it that can make you stronger. No pain, no gain. The key is to **force** yourself to find the silver lining in the dark cloud and to examine how that event can motivate you to be a better and wiser person.

Remember that everyone experiences pain, heartache and evil at some point. What distinguishes those who stay stuck versus those who overcome and grow is how they respond to it, not the event itself. Use the simple formula:

Event + Response to Event = Outcome

You cannot control the events of your life to a large extent, but you can control how you choose to respond to them. Your power lies in your decision to respond positively. You do have a choice because you are what you think about. I challenge you to use negativity as opportunities to grow, problem-solve and gain wisdom for future relationships. Now let's get busy! I'll do the first one for you in case you need a guide.

Major Event

I dated a woman who I really thought I had great chemistry with. We would laugh, talk and listen to each other for hours. At the time, we were both going through a lot and found each other to be great emotional resources. However, after four months the relationship lost its passion and fire. Once we both started doing better, we lost the will to spend time with one another. How could something so promising die all of a sudden?

Life Lesson

I guess neediness is not the structure to build a lasting relationship on. In reality, we were great friends who bonded to help one another overcome. Additionally, utilizing sex to heal and support your partner may feel good but it can easily confuse you. Somehow sex was mistaken for long lasting love.

In retrospect, we should have abstained and built a relationship on friendship by using conversation, prayer and fun activities to support one another. From now on, friends should remain friends by practicing platonic intimacy and waiting until marriage to engage in sex that would permanently bond us so that no one got hurt or confused.

Silver Lining

Thank God that we both felt the same way so that neither party felt used, and we were able to maintain our friendship.

Also, I do appreciate meeting and sharing some wonderful times with an awesome person. I am happy that I learned this life lesson so that I can be more self-disciplined so that I can move into a relationship headed for marriage where we can have all the sex we desire because we are permanently bonded by the spirit and vows we took.

How Can I Respond So It Makes Me A Stronger Person?

From now on, instead of relying solely on a long-time friend for support, I will fill my times of loneliness, despair and hopelessness with prayer, platonic friends and helping others so that I am able to enter into the next relationship whole, healed and aware of my blind spots.

Did that help? I hope so. Now it's your time. Let the healing begin.

Major Event One

I dated a man that I believed to be the "One". I met him through mutual friends that respected and he studied me for a long time or 1 yr. before he pursued me.

Life Lesson

just because I met him through mutual friends does not mean it is a great match like they are.

Silver Lining

He also knows that we were growing apart. I believe he just did not want it to end when it did.

How Can I Respond So It Makes Me A Stronger Person?

I need to build a stronger foundation and communicate more effectively next time of what is expected.

Major Event Two

Life Lesson

____

____

____

Silver Lining

____

____

____

How Can I Respond So It Makes Me A Stronger Person?

____

____

____

Major Event Three

____

____

____

Life Lesson

____

____

____

Silver Lining

____

____

____

How Can I Respond So It Makes Me A Stronger Person?

____

____

____

I hope that these exercises are helping to facilitate the healing process. It's important that we heal before we enter into our next relationship and unload unnecessary baggage on undeserving partners. Remember, you are what you think about it. So, continue finding the positive in each stressful situation so that you can ultimately control your growth. This is where a relationship with God and understanding the divine relationship between pain, love and growth will benefit your soul and ability to grow and experience joy through hardship.

I must credit Dr. Charles Stanley (intouch.org) and Bishop Dale C. Bronner (woffamily.org) and their teachings for helping me through my own negative events and coming out more powerful, joyful and trusting in God's will for my life.

I encourage you to seek these teachers out as well and initiate any form of counseling, coaching and guided prayer necessary to help you in your own journey of healing. Remember that someone has already been where you are and come out a wiser, happier, and more fulfilled person as a result. Follow their path so that you can be a victor versus a victim.

I love you, God loves you and I want you to experience the fullness of everything positive that God has for you without wasting another moment of debilitating despair when you can be growing, healing and ultimately loving God's plan for your life. Feel free to reach out to me (www.drtartt.com) to help with these exercises and lead you to more resources.

Finally, love is a DECISION not a feeling. Thus, in order to overcome insecurity you must make the life changing decision to **decide** to love yourself first. God's love is unconditional and, thus, is not based on past mistakes, sin, weight, dress size, height, maturity, beauty, finances, skin color, ethnicity, cup size or any other material item you can think of.

My friends, the wonderful reality is that God loves you through it all and there is absolutely nothing that you can do to change that for as long as you shall live. If you don't know him then I encourage you to get to know him because God's love is stronger than any feeling you will ever experience and has the power to elevate you above heartbreak, loneliness and insecurity. Don't you owe it to yourself to develop a life-long love for yourself today?

Let's get started right now. In this final section, I want you to write yourself a love letter. Why? Quite simply, how you can expect a man to write you a love letter if you don't know what there is about you to love in the first place? Thus, pull out your pen and start writing the kind of love letter that you deserve to yourself. If you cannot find the words, get on your knees, pray and ask God to guide your pen as you craft the most wonderful love letter known to mankind. Decide to love yourself today.

Dear Alondra,

I love you.

I love how you like to smile and uplift others. I love how you will pray for others no matter whats going on. I love your resilience. I love how passionate you are and nurturing you are. I love how you are there when needed. I love how you keep yourself and others going. I love your laugh. I love your mind.

Formula THREE

CONFIDENCE IS MANDATORY! YOU BETTER "WOW" HIM

"Men are driven towards a woman's attraction power which is all about *attitude*." Possessing a phenomenal attitude about yourself is essential to your self-development because it will help you embrace your inherent greatness. To step into your greatness, begin by focusing 100 percent on your inner beauty and creating the magnetic attraction power to which men are forced to yield.

Men are addicted to women's beauty. In fact, advertisers use it to sell liquor, cars, deodorant and even razor blades. Men are slaves to both the visual and the tactile. These senses are developed as early as infancy. Baby boys love to stare at their mothers, who represent the most beautiful being they know. They love to look into their eyes, feel their face and touch their hair; therefore, it is only natural that these senses heighten during puberty and become dominant in manhood.

There is not a single man alive who can resist looking at a beautiful woman; luckily, social etiquette restricts his desire to touch her without permission. Nevertheless, regardless of the prevailing stereotype, men are not only attracted to a woman's physical beauty but to her positive mental and emotional attitude and overall attraction power.

Nothing is more appealing than women who feel beautiful and emit an aura of self-confidence and supreme power to attract the men of their choice. For some reason, however, countless women fail to utilize this inherent power and, instead, singularly focus on their physical beauty. The complete beauty of women encompasses the mind, body and soul. Women who understand this are total packages.

Whether dressed to the nines for a night out on the town, draped in an emotion-thrilling teddy or sipping from a water bottle in a jogging suit, women still emit an aura of feminine power that men simply cannot resist. These women go far beyond being just another pretty face. Men recognize a total package as soon as she enters the room and, simultaneously, focus all their attention on wooing her.

How can you harness this power? The secret is simple, yet the application is complex. It is all about having a positive mental and emotional attitude, something over which you have 100% control. A positive mental and emotional attitude is contagious and immediately sets you apart from others who have not cultivated its magnetic effect. This type of attitude makes things happen, and success tends to fall into your lap.

Men will go out of their way to smile and say hello. Passersby can't help but turn their heads, and even accompanied men feel the urge to sneak a peek. Once you master the power of a positive mental and emotional attitude, there is no longer a need to think of other women as competition. Bystanders in heels and cute dresses are just extras in your movie, and you are the megastar!

God made you beautiful, but it is up to you to embrace your beauty and use it to attract MR. RIGHT. Take control and lure him! You shouldn't have to pretend to be anything you are not—just be the total package that God created you to be, and men will respond.

I met a total package by the name of Karen a few years ago. The first time we met, I commented, "You think you're beautiful, don't you?"

Without hesitation, she responded, "No, Alduan, I'm convinced, and so are you."

"Wow" was all I could think because she was right. She was in absolute control from the first interaction, and I followed her lead and gladly submitted to her power. Karen was a woman of beauty who had harnessed the power of the law of attraction to get any man she chose. Let me tell you how she did it.

I first met Karen in, of all places, Las Vegas, Nevada, during a 100 Black Men of America conference. I was working on a youth project, and she was on vacation. I met her as I was walking through Bally's Casino on my way to an afternoon seminar. One smile from Karen stopped me in my tracks. I looked around to see if she was alone, but before I could complete my surveillance, she motioned me over.

I was caught off guard a little, but Karen was so cool and confident that I just went with the flow—her flow. She was already in control. She flashed a radiant smile, confidently introduced herself, and asked me if I could help her understand the rules of the craps table. She asked my name and my reason for wearing a business suit in Las Vegas. I'll admit that her swagger made me put up my guard, so I hesitated because I was unsure of her intentions. After all, I was in Vegas and one has to wonder, "What's the hustle?"

I asked for her line of business, and she matter-of-factly replied, "Oh, I'm a therapist."

"Yeah, right," I thought, "*I'm* the therapist." At this point, I bet you are thinking the same thing I was. If she was conducting therapy, she only had male clients.

I was tempted to run the whole "Listen-baby-I'm-from-Atlanta-GA-and-I-know-a-hustle-when-I-see-one" line, but my instincts stopped me. There was something intriguing about Karen that was too sincere and genuine to fit that line of work. My curiosity was piqued, and I decided to be late for my seminar.

It was a good decision because Karen was certainly Lady Luck, and I won a lot of money at the craps table. After about an hour of doubling and tripling my money, another man came over and asked whether she was OK. Karen smiled and indicated that she was fine. He left as quickly as he approached, and she continued to place bets. Now I was sure that I was being hustled.

When I inquired about her "sponsor," she laughed and told me that he was a friend who wanted a travel companion to relax with in Las Vegas. OK, now it was time for the brother-from-Atlanta line. I figured that I would just as well keep my earnings before the hustle and expose her. After all, I could still catch the last half of my meeting.

"Karen, baby, let me see your license to practice therapy in California. You should know you can't hustle a brother from Hotlanta, where fast hustles are a way of life."

Karen smiled, nonchalantly reached in her Chanel bag, and showed me her license. I was thoroughly confused because things just were not adding up.

I looked around for the sponsor, and he was talking to other females, appearing to have a great time doing it too. Therefore, you know what I thought next; Karen and her sponsor were swingers! I decided to push the envelope and just ask her as she was sipping on a cocktail. Her reaction confirmed that this was no Vegas hustle. She spit out her drink and looked offended.

"First, Alduan, what gives you the idea that I want to be with either one of you? I thought you were cute, and you looked intelligent, so I asked you to keep me company, but you are killing my buzz with your paranoid questions. Are you part of the 100 or the FBI? Chill dude...and shouldn't you be heading to your meeting?" She certainly knew how to deflate my balloon.

I was embarrassed and stunned that Karen had the gall to think she could just dismiss me like some annoying gnat. I was not about to leave this puzzle unsolved and decided to leave on my own terms. I suggested that she provide her number, so we could finish this discussion later. Without making eye contact, she whipped out her phone and beamed her number to my phone. When the sound cued us that the process was complete, Karen flashed that million-dollar smile and in a sweet, sexy way, encouraged me to only use the number when I decided I was in need of having *"some fun."* She tugged at the lapels of my sports coat and together we laughed because she was clearly playing with me about my escort, swinger and hustler references. Even though I was embarrassed, she knew just how to give me a soft jab in the ribs without drawing blood.

To her credit, Karen had "IT": a positive mental and emotional attitude, physical appeal and supreme attraction power. She knew I was going to call and reveled in her power. I'll confess that I was extremely intrigued and actually enjoyed no longer being in control. I was so caught up in trying to figure out why I wanted to spend more time with Karen that I couldn't even concentrate during the seminar. After all, she lived on the other side of the world, and she already had a "friend." Here I was, surrounded by beautiful women swarming around the conference and hotel who were poised to use their own attraction powers to recruit a successful executive, yet I was consumed with thoughts of only Karen.

As instructed, I dutifully called Karen after a late-dinner reception and left a message that my friends and I were headed to a party. She text-messaged me back, "Have fun. I'm just starting dinner. Will call you later." I figured it was a brush-off and that she was flirting with some other unsuspecting sucker. It didn't matter, though. I had not seen my friends from other chapters of the 100 Black Men in years, and I was ready to have a great time. My group convinced another large party of conference attendees to party with us and have some fun.

If there is any "best" advantage to being a member of the 100 Black Men and attending the national conference, it's that there are just as many women who attend as men. It makes sense. What better place is there to search for eligible men than at an all-male national conference? Before long, we were forty-to-fifty deep inside the club, having the time of our lives.

I was dancing with two women at the same time and felt like I was living a rap video. My swagger and confidence were at an all-time high, and I was feeding off the energy, the success of the chapter, and the much-needed attention after recently coming out of a very painful relationship.

As the night went on, I kept checking my phone to see if Karen had called, but I stopped looking around 11:00 PM. There were so many desirable women in the club that night that I had more than enough options. Suddenly, I felt my phone vibrate and wondered who could be calling me at 1:15 AM. It was Karen.

Her text read, "Alduan, ready to have some fun? Had a great meal and a killer nap. Where are you?"

I responded, "Club Risqué in the Paris Hotel."

Within ten minutes she texted me again. "I'm downstairs—which bar?"

"The side bar."

After about fifteen minutes, it dawned on me that she needed someone to let her into our section, and I tried to locate the bouncer. Before I could find him, Karen walked in escorted by the bouncer! She entered the room as if she were making her debut on the red carpet at the Academy Awards. All eyes were on her. The two young women who were dancing with me expeditiously moved to the side.

Karen walked right up to them and, in typical Karen fashion, commanded the room by complimenting them on their outfits. She struck up a genuine conversation with them, and after about ten minutes with Karen, they were all laughing and having a good time.

For those of you who know the dynamics of female interactions, ten minutes is an eternity for women to converse with the "competition." Karen, however, didn't view the other women as competition. She saw them as gorgeous women who had their stuff together. She hugged her new "friends" and asked me if I was ready to "burn rubber." I hesitated just for a moment because my boys and I were kicking it hard, but I simply couldn't resist. Bowing out gracefully, I informed my boys that I would see them the next day. Equally intrigued and mesmerized, the look in their eyes said, "Who is *she*?" I tried to play it cool, like she was an old friend or a colleague from the West coast. Inside, I was bursting with excitement.

The most surprising thing was the other two women smiled at Karen and told her to have fun. I was confused. Had I been bought? This was getting weirder by the moment. I started to ask Karen what she said to the other women but remembered that I had already stuck my foot in my mouth by asking too many questions earlier in the day.

We went to another club and danced until five AM. We didn't even have to pay to get in. They all seemed to know her and just let us cut the line without flashing credentials or money. Not only were the men mesmerized, but even the women asked her who she was. People came over to our table all night, one after another, trying to figure out who she was.

I was wondering too and was listening every time they asked. Before long, it became clear that Karen was just a phenomenal woman with a celebrity attitude who was convinced of her inner and outer beauty. As we caught a cab back to the hotel to have breakfast before parting ways, I asked if she was aware of what she had. She smiled and responded confidently, "Of course."

She went on to explain that, at one point in her life, she let a man define her. She based her whole existence on whether he was happy with her. She dieted for him, changed her job, resisted her urge to spend time with her female friends, and did not travel despite having a strong case of wanderlust.

As it turned out, her boyfriend still cheated on her with another female who didn't even measure up to the beauty standards he had set for Karen. She made a vow after that relationship to love herself unconditionally and share that love with the world. She explained, "I learned to embrace God's beauty within me and feed off the beauty in others."

Karen disclosed that God had revealed her calling shortly after that devastating relationship—to use her beautiful spirit to reveal and promote the beauty and love within others. She explained that the best way for her to do that was to purposely radiate beauty and love into the world. It was amazing to learn what made Karen such a wonderful person and why she was a powerful and inspiring therapist.

In my lifetime, I have met hundreds of women with the same mindset as Karen, but the qualities that made her unique were her supreme confidence and the complete absence of self-doubt. She had a way of radiating beauty from within and drawing it out of others. She had a genuine gift for interacting with people without appearing the least bit arrogant, snide or negative. Karen was definitely a total package because of her positive mental and emotional attitude. She was the epitome of a woman of beauty.

There were other beautiful women in Vegas that weekend, but few could compare to Karen. While others preferred to focus on physical beauty to attract the opposite sex, Karen unleashed her spiritual beauty and welcomed both men and women to be drawn to her positive spirit. Karen is a living example of how to attract love by first being the giver. She put so much positive energy and love into the world that she could not help but get it right back!

Karen represents the full beauty found within all women. True beauty is not merely about outward appearance that will fade with time. It's about inner beauty that emits and radiates rays of positively charged influence throughout the world. Karen loved people so much that they had to love her back. She did not view other women as "competition," and avoided comparing her beauty to others. Instead, she acknowledged their beauty, and in turn, they responded graciously and gave her full acceptance. She looked at the world through beauty-coated eyes, embraced it, and complimented it in a way that made people feel recognized and loved.

Karen's influence on my way of thinking about beauty was so profound that I had to dedicate this entire chapter to her. I am compelled to share her lesson with you.

The lesson is that you must believe you are as beautiful as you say you are. The key is to fall deeply in love with yourself, not in a self-absorbed way, but in a way that allows you to project a positive mental and emotional attitude that will enable you to eliminate negativity and self-doubt while focusing on projecting beauty into the world. Once you learn this, you will continuously attract the quality attention, love and respect you are due. Let your magnificent inner glow permeate your world, and you will never have a problem attracting MR. RIGHT.

Application Section

There are many people who understand this chapter but struggle to apply it. Theoretically, it sounds good but when left to their own devices, they still get caught up in female competitiveness, gossiping and disparaging others in an effort to make themselves feel good. I certainly understand the rationale behind the behavior- bring others down so that you can rise up. However, it should be noted that the rationale is flawed. I strongly suggest that anyone who is using that theory to immediately stop and replace it with the one I am about to disclose.

The key to attracting more love into your life is to follow God's model. God loves you unconditionally the very second you are consummated. Actually, that's not entirely accurate because he loved you *before* you were conceived.

The Creator created you as a product of His love which means that you are love already. The problem is that many of us seek love without ever seeking the only source that truly fulfills that desire. How can you really know yourself without having relationship with the Love from which you were created? God is Love!

I'm not a preacher (yet) and respect everyone's decision to choose their spiritual path. I simply want women all over the world to know that they are loved, regardless of color, religious affiliation, ethnicity, size, shape or class. It pains me to see people (especially women) wander through life feeling unloved, disconnected and lacking.

No matter what literature they read, they still cannot figure out how to love themselves or others and, thus, project and illicit an evil spirit which further convinces them of the inherit evil in the world. For those of you of who struggle with this, are you willing to explore the reason for feeling less than the person you were created to be?

You may feel like less than the person God intends for you to be because you have yet to tap into the source that enables you to find your purpose for being, which is to love. Love, for you, is illusive because you have yet to use your full ability to transfer this love to others. Without love, we serve no purpose and cannot positively impact the world. However, the second you decide to enter into relationship with God, the source of all love, you will experience a sense of self-love, joy and inner fulfillment like you've never known before.

You will begin to shake off depression, past abuse, abandonment, rejection and failed relationships because they no longer have the power from stopping you from giving and creating the love you desire in your life. You are connected to the source.

If you want to test God's love then might I suggest that you simply emulate Him and the way he loves? Instead of waiting on others to love you before you love them, I encourage you to love them unconditionally. That's right, just like Karen.

Have you ever thrown a boomerang? What happens when you hurl it? It comes right back to you. The more force you apply when you throw it, the greater range it has. By contrast, if you only use a little force it will fail to go anywhere.

I want to encourage you to throw your boomerang every single day of your life. If you truly want control over your love life then you must always make the first move! When you enter a room, forcefully spread love throughout the room. Compliment everyone you see. If you can't figure out what to say, simply tell them what you want them to ultimately say to you.

You are in control of what message you send with your boomerang. If you want more love then throw out (give) more love first. For those of you who are "waiting" on love, shame on you (Smile)! If I hear, "The Lord is going to send me a man" one more time I might start giving this book away! God didn't wait to love you so why would you stand stagnant, boomerang in hand, and not throw yours first? You reap what you sow right? So, why would you think that God is going to "send you a man" when you are at home...waiting, eating dinner alone with your boomerang?

Get out of the house and throw that boomerang all around town. You will never be faulted for displaying too much love. Men all around the world are complaining that they feel unnoticed, under-appreciated and unwanted. They mask their tears with affairs, drugs, alcohol, obsessing about their physical bodies, trying to be millionaires, work and searching for love with their penis instead of their hearts. Look around my beautiful ladies, men are crying all over the world. Won't you share your boomerang with one today?

I'm serious, despite my smiling as I just typed that last sentence. You will *never* experience problems with getting the attention you deserve if you take CONTROL and speak to men first. Don't worry about feeling desperate, too forward or overly flirtatious. There is a process and it works well. Remember that men need you to make the first move out of common courtesy. Men have learned the hard way that they cannot approach every woman they see. She has to first give him permission or he's in for a rude response and rejection. Thus, men have become astute at reading your body language.

What does your body language convey to men? Trust me, you are being observed daily by men who want to approach you. How easy do you make it for a quality man to make your acquaintance so they can ask you out to dinner? Many women desire quality companionship while their body language conveys the complete opposite. Make sure that your body language conveys positive thoughts and feelings.

I know you might be tired, frustrated and annoyed by being single but you should never show it! Every time you leave the house you should advertise a great woman who is open to the suitor is willing to pay top dollar in quality time, love, and consistent caring for his future wife.

The simplest, classiest and most effective way to share your boomerang and control the attention you seek is to smile and make quick, glancing eye contact. However, you must prepare yourself for this interaction before you even leave the house. Men are adept at distinguishing between a reactive versus a natural smile. If you smile only because you see a man versus wearing a smile naturally, you'll fail to convey authenticity and appear pressed.

This is what women do who have "IT". They are always full of love, ready to serve and walk in expectation that their love will be reciprocated. Here's a secret too... "IT" women have been cheated on, abused, lied to, under-appreciated, etc. in their past too, but they never stopped throwing their boomerangs! Stop making excuses about why you won't show love first and rely on God to give you discernment as to whose advances you should receive.

When you proactively give love, as God does, then the men will find you. The world is a lonely place and men need all the love they can get. What did you say? I heard you, you are questioning as to whether this love will be appreciated and reciprocated? You know psychologists can hear voices (smile). Allow God to be your guide and let the man's behavior provide signs that you are sufficiently valued enough for you to continuously share your romantic boomerang with him.

When you have "IT" there will be a plethora of suitors for you to choose from. All you have to do is pick the best fit. What a wonderful problem to have, huh?

Let's practice attracting the type of attention and love that you desire to your life now by doing a few exercises. After all, you are not getting any younger and if you put these exercises into practice you might just attract a quality suitor just in time for the holidays, your birthday or summer vacation. Let's get busy. Men are waiting to make your acquaintance.

Creating Love (Boomerang) Exercises

Within the last week, how many opportunities have you passed up to share your boomerang with others (male or female)? List them.

1) ____

____

____

2)

____

____

____

3) ____

____

____

Those three opportunities represent three connections you could have made this week alone. Just for a second, think about how good you would have felt if three people would have taken the time to connect with you this week. Well, if you want that feeling then you must be willing to give that very same feeling (at the same intensity) to others first.

Starting right now, I want you to do two things. First, I want you to immediately connect with someone close to you right now. I want you to either visit them in person or contact them via the phone and tell them the things that you most appreciate about them and list their best qualities. After you finish, I want you write down how they responded and how it made you feel as well.

One of the most rewarding feelings is giving versus always receiving it. This is why God loves us no matter what we do. He is a giver not a taker. What you should experience is that you derive more pleasure and satisfaction from making others feel loved. Additionally, you will find that your loved ones will reciprocate your kind words and return the favor. Don't believe me; test your boomerang theory yourself. Complete the following exercise now.

Friend ***1)*** ______________________________

Their Response:

____

____

____

How Did You Feel?

____

____

____

Friend *2)* ______________________________________

Their Response:

____

____

____

How Did You Feel?

____

____

____

Friend *3)* ________________________________

Their Response:

____

____

____

How Did You Feel?

____

____

____

Second, I want you to do the same thing with three total strangers this week. Simply, rely on your intuition to pick the right people and invest your energy in making them feel good about themselves. You can compliment their attire, smile, beautiful spirit, etc. while genuinely showing love without the condition of it being returned.

Remember, you will receive the same energy that you give so make sure you think positively and give them all that you have. There really is no need to be afraid. After all, who in this world doesn't need to hear a compliment, encouraging word, or praise from time to time?

Trust your instinct! People are emotionally starving for companionship, a sense of connection and unconditional, Godly love. You are not selling insurance, swamp land or devalued real estate. You are simply spreading love and trusting God (not that particular person) to return love in some form or fashion later. Newton's third law of motion states that *for every action, there is an equal and opposite reaction*. This means that when you give love that it will be returned (opposition direction/back to you) with the same intensity that you gave it. Additionally, if you desire to receive more love then you must take action by giving the love you desire first.

Test the theory yourself by making a pledge to do this each week. Watch and enjoy your circle of friends, sense of self-worth and connection with others increase in proportion to how much love you show. I am so excited about the results you will soon experience. So, don't wait. Get busy now and make your pledge to yourself right now.

How many strangers do you pledge to share your boomerang with each week?

PERSONAL PLEDGE:

I, ____________________________, pledge to share my boomerang

with at least _____ people each week.

Signed,

____

Dated:

____

Finding Love Exercises

Now that you have pledged to increase your friendship circle, let's get started on finding that man you deserve! Remember that what you see is what you'll be. Hence, the first step in attracting a man is to create him and the experience you desire with him in your head. This is another autosuggestion exercise and one I'm sure that you will enjoy.

Exercise 1

I want you to envision a beautiful, happy, fun, and confident woman. Take one minute to close your eyes and create a detailed image of this woman. What does she wear? How does she smell? What does she think about herself? What does she love most about herself? Now, you can open your eyes. I want you to describe this woman using as much detail as you can.

____

____

____

____

____

____

Now, use the description from above to guide you as you create this image in *your* mirror. You are that beautiful woman you just envisioned! You may need to visit the boutique or utilize that walk-in closet of yours to find all of the accessories that you need. Every woman's style is different but find what makes you feel beautiful and clothe yourself as a queen. Play some soft music, light some candles and dim the lights to set the mood and begin the process of falling madly in love with yourself. Now, I want you to take a picture to capture the moment and place it on the next page to serve as a daily reminder of your inherent beauty.

It's okay to admire yourself and fall in love with God's creation. When you learn to see yourself as beautiful first, then men will see what you see- beauty. When they stare and compliment you on how beautiful you are you will believe it and act accordingly. You will be able to transcend the pressure of settling for less than what you deserve and questioning your worth. The evidence will always reside on the next page as well as in the reflection in your man's eyes, and it will **always** be beautiful.

GREAT MEN LOVE ME

Insert Your Photo Here

Now doesn't that picture look beautiful! How can men not fall in love with you? The truth is that men do love you. You just have to make sure you pick the right one who desires to appreciate versus destroy a woman's beauty. Regardless of what any man says, the truth is that men need your beauty in their lives.

A world without women lacks beauty and, thus, is cold, uninspiring and lonely. This is why single men get intoxicated with even the sight of a beautiful woman who is convinced of her own beauty. Men need your permanent beauty in their lives. Without your love, men feel like their lives are incomplete. Why? Your beauty serves as a reminder to him that his world is beautiful. No matter how ugly the people treat him at work or how much money he loses or how much negativity he faces, he can always come home to the ONE woman he can always depend on to be his living flower and brighten his life.

Men Do Need You

Exercise 2: Now that I have hopefully convinced you of how much men desperately need you, let us begin to attract that man into your life.

I want you to imagine that the man you desire is staring at you as you admire your own beauty in the mirror. Write out what you desire him to say, feel and think about you. Make sure that you write with emotion to evoke the intensity of the interaction that you desire. Be sure to include compliments about your character and your physical appearance.

Wow. Alondra is the most beautiful woman inside and out that I have ever laid eyes on. I love this woman so much. with her fine and loving self. I can just breathe her in. God I love the way she makes me feel. I know this is the only woman for me, my lifelong partner, mother of my children. She is so amazing!. I love everything about her, even her flaws. My baby loves me and I love her.

Great job! Now it's time to make those visualization a reality! Since you are already dressed and mentally prepared, I want you to pick the date that you choose to share your beauty with the world. No matter how beautiful you are or how much value you add to man, he cannot see you unless you leave home. A man cannot admire a rose that he cannot see.

If you are truly ready for change now, your Doctor's orders are to leave the house and attract the very interaction that you just described. Right now, this may sound bold, daring and challenging but that's exactly what men like—a bold, daring and confident woman who takes no prisoners when she walks and struts her beauty because she is focused on opportunity versus failure.

I can feel it! Some of you are fired up and already making plans. Others of you, however, are still questioning your beauty and my sanity! I still love you because you still look beautiful with that sour face you're giving me right now. Let me explain the psychology behind why this exercise will work so that you don't delay the process any further.

The visualization exercises that I am giving you are based on the psychological principle of auto-suggestion. Autosuggestion is the process by which an individual trains the subconscious mind to believe something, or systematically schematizes the person's own mental associations, usually for a given purpose.

This technique has been used by the majority of highly successful people in this world who understand and harness the power of creating their desired life in their head and taking immediate, daily action in order to realize it.

Make no mistakes about it. Taking action on attracting the love that you desire is a decision. Autosuggestion will work but only if you commit to the process and believe. You will never to able to perceive something that you cannot see, feel, hear, smell or touch. Thus, it is important that you develop a positive attitude and behave with an air of expectation if you are to attract Mr. Right into your life.

Be the change that you wish to create in your life. Stop waiting and start attracting more of what you desire and it will become reality. Keep your confidence up; expect to hear those beautiful words that you just wrote from a handsome, well-dressed man with a melodic deep voice that soothes your soul this week.

I am giving you permission to create the life, companionship and love that you desire and deserve. Of course, be wise, safe and use sound judgment when you step out on the town. Send me an email and let me know how this is working for you so I can share with fellow readers as evidence that this really does work (Drtartt@drtartt.com).

Formula FOUR

STAY IN YOUR LANE AND PLEASE ... DON'T CRITICIZE HIS DRIVING! (THERE IS POWER IN SUBMISSION)

"How can your man lead if you want to be the man too?" The first book in the *Bible*, Genesis, tells the story of how man and woman were created. Adam was created first to wander the Earth; however, God states, "It is not good for the man to be alone. I will make a helper suitable for him." Therefore, he created woman out of the body of Adam. The story describes God sinking Adam into a deep sleep and removing his rib to make his soul mate, Eve. *Genesis* reads, "This is now bone of my bones and flesh of my flesh; she shall be called 'woman' for she was taken out of man."

From the beginning of civilization, there is evidence that God created men and women to be perfect complements for one another. Man fortifies woman and vice versa; however, God was very clear on the position that each plays in regard to the relationship. Thus, there is divine wisdom inherent in the idea that behind (beside) every strong man stands a strong woman. The operative word is *beside* because it clearly assigns the woman to a position of support versus subordination in the relationship.

God assigned gender roles to maintain harmonious relations among men and women. However, some women have taken offense at being assigned to be behind their men, and feel they legitimately belong alongside, or even in front of, their men. This is a tragic and colossal mistake because it disrupts the divine order of relationships according to God's plan. With divorce and marital discord at all-time highs, it is clear that something is flawed with modern-day male-female relations.

Modern society reflects a lack of understanding of God's word. Overzealous wings of the feminist movement flew too far past the true goal of women's empowerment and inappropriately into an attack on men.

Changing times have appropriately changed the role of women in society and the workplace but totally confused them at home. Home is a place of comfort and harmony, and they don't exist when there are frequent battles for power. Likewise, an increasing number of men are experienced arrested development and deem themselves incapable of leading a relationship. They desire the title but lack the skill.

The core of the conflict lies in the reality that no healthy relationship can have two leaders. For the relationship to be healthy, the man must assume the leadership position. If the woman assumes this role, she inevitably steps out of her lane and right into the path of conflict.

Similar to the sport of track, when a lane violation occurs, one of two things happens next: You apologize and move back into your lane, or you get pushed out of the way. Men are sensitive creatures and want to accept their instinctive roles as protectors, providers and leaders. If they are subordinated to that role, they lose their sense of purpose and seek relationships that are more in tune with their basic instinct and ego that need to lead.

Single women grossly outnumber single men and, thus, certainly desire to have harmonious relations when they meet an eligible bachelor. However, women also desire to be treated with respect and valued for the many talents they bring into relationships. In fact, it is common for women to make more money, be sounder financial investors and be better overall decision makers.

Thus, conflict is inherent as the ultimate dilemma is created. Women can either assert their superior skills and lose their man or revert to pre-feminist times to please their men while devaluing themselves. This begs the question: How can women both support their men and be assertive at the same time?

My fifth grade art teacher used to say, "Alduan, it's all in the technique." So what is the technique to feeling empowered without offending men? How can you submit without losing your voice and power? The key is to wait patiently and lead from the side until he invites you to take the helm. This is a lesson Latoya had to learn the hard way.

Latoya was five-feet-five; a petite woman with an attitude the size of King Kong. Her DKNY power business suits, brown-leather Coach brief case, and $300 shoes all alluded to her success. Her stride projected all the confidence in the world. Her skirts were always professionally appropriate but intentionally revealed her supremely sculpted calf muscles. She was a high-powered attorney working for a large-size firm in New York. She developed a reputation for devouring the competition quickly without regard or remorse for their position. In the legal world, Latoya was the best. She quickly established a name for herself and was on the fast track to partner status. With her professional life ascending, all that was missing was a great man with whom she could settle down.

She met a gentleman by the name of JP at a social mixer during the Martin Luther King holiday weekend whom she hoped would fit the bill. JP was a 6-foot tall man with a slim body. He had an exotic look: His curly hair, wing-shaped eyes, and distinct cheekbones hinted of Native American origins. He impressed Latoya with his blue pinstriped three-piece suit, polished Cole Hahn shoes and quick wit. JP owned a line of urban clothing stores and was recognized throughout the community as a self-made man.

The two connected immediately, and before they knew it,

they were celebrating their one-year anniversary. Together, they made one heck of a power couple since money was the last thing that stressed either of them. In fact, they were contemplating marriage, but both had concerns. While their respective success led to a great financial position, it produced more than its share of power struggles and interpersonal conflict.

They were growing concerned about the frequency of their arguments and wondered if they could succeed at marriage. Both had friends who had married and divorced within only a few years. Neither JP nor Latoya wanted to replicate the pattern of divorce and decided to live together and, instead, to simulate marriage. They shared household expenses and even established a joint bank account.

Before long, they were arguing over almost everything: investment strategies, theoretical child-rearing practices, gender roles and work schedules. It appeared that the longer they remained together, the more they began to dislike one another's company. This was a major problem because the friendship that so solidly bonded them was quickly eroding and compromising the relationship. Like so many relationships, the basic arguments centered on a mutual desire for more control and power.

JP frequently accused Latoya of being disrespectful and too strong for her own good. "And I'm gonna stay *too strong for my own good* until the day I die," Latoya would often retort.

In retrospect, she should have said, "until the day we break up" because that is exactly what happened shortly after JP proposed to her. JP figured that the arguments stemmed from Latoya's need to solidify their future relationship, so he produced a sparkling two-carat princess-cut diamond ring on her thirtieth birthday. When the arguments continued despite his proposal, he became frustrated, disappointed and hopeless that she would ever be the type of wife he desired. JP asked for the ring back and moved out.

Latoya was devastated and baffled. Where did things go wrong? What happened to make JP leave so abruptly after proposing? The entire time they were dating, JP was a model of consistency and stability. Pushing her to the side suddenly and abruptly departing would be out of character. Latoya decided to put her pain and pride aside and do something that men often wished more women would do. She decided to self-reflect and explore JP's perspective, hoping to find the correct lane to exist in JP's life.

Her first step was to listen to JP's desires and expectations for a spouse. When she did, she learned things about JP that she never knew. While they had spent months discussing her specific needs and desires, she had never practiced reciprocity to explore those of JP. She was somewhat embarrassed to admit that she never even thought about his needs. She was too absorbed in her own world.

She learned that JP was searching for a woman who really wanted to have his back through thick and thin. His ideal wife would demonstrate her loyalty by providing unconditional love and support regardless of the circumstances. He had listened to his partners complain about frequent arguments and control battles and decided he would rather be unmarried than argue for the rest of his life. He wanted a woman who wanted to submit, and he looked forward to being the man Latoya desired him to be; however, he clearly saw love as a two-way street and was not about to engage in another one-sided love affair. Additionally, he was very traditional and wanted his spouse to be biblically submissive, recognizing and appreciating his duty toward leadership within the relationship.

Latoya was actually receptive to respecting traditional gender roles and was "OK" with the basic idea of submission. Her parents practiced similar gender roles; however, problems arose when she privately began attaching qualifiers to them. As long as JP made what she valued as "wise" decisions, she would follow his lead. For example, JP and Latoya had very different views about how to invest their money. Latoya chose a more conservative approach and wanted to invest in mutual funds and stocks. JP, desiring to retire early, was more aggressive and wanted to invest in real estate.

Latoya was a savvy businesswoman, having the experience of handling securities cases as well as being the daughter of a Wall Street CEO. Her father warned her that the condominium real estate market was overdeveloped and likely headed for a fall. JP respected Latoya's input but saw too much opportunity in a new neighborhood in a trendy part of town to pass up.

His plan was to buy numerous condominiums early in the construction phase, upgrade them before the prices increased and sell them when the neighborhood appreciated. At thirty-three, he figured he would generate enough revenue in the next few years so that Latoya could stay home with their future children for a few years without being financially strapped.

JP and Latoya's newly created joint account turned out to be just the test they were looking for to assess potential long-term conflict. They argued daily about whose investment strategy to follow. "Baby, I need you to trust me and support what I do without being a dream killer," JP would complain.

"JP, you can lose all the money you want, but I work too hard to throw it away on some get rich quick scheme," Latoya would warn.

Eventually, Latoya stopped contributing to the joint account and set up her own account without even discussing it with him. This greatly offended JP because he was widely recognized in the community as a successful entrepreneur and was not used to being so openly questioned, abandoned and disrespected. Additionally, didn't she realize that he was doing this for her?

Despite being deeply in love with Latoya, JP took her withdrawal from the joint account to be a major offense and a serious red flag. While he disagreed with what he deemed to be Latoya's overly conservative investment strategy and felt strongly about real estate, he respected her too much to make his own moves. He went along with the separation of their accounts to avoid further conflict but, in his mind, the damage had already been done. After all, he really had no choice but to consent because Latoya had already withdrawn her money and trust.

He decided to follow his gut and invest in real estate in an effort to double his income over the next few years. Despite her disapproval, JP was surprised when Latoya refused even to tour the properties to lend her input, support or emotional backing toward his success. He understood, on some level, how she would not trust him with money since he had similar concerns himself, but not to support him, even after her finances were protected, was inexcusable and un-wifely.

In four months, Latoya's father's words proved prophetic as the condominium market came barreling to a halt. JP was now stuck with three high-priced condominium mortgages that were actually depreciating due to oversupply in an economic recession.

JP was distraught, but felt he could not turn to Latoya for support. He wanted to acknowledge that she was right but her self-righteous attitude and his masculine pride would not allow him. Latoya seemed to bask in her success and during an argument she sneered, "You should let me handle the business from now on."

Deeply hurt and embarrassed, it was at that moment that JP's love for Latoya died. Within two weeks, he moved out to reside in one of his condominiums and refused to return her calls. In her presence, he avoided eye contact, and his attitude turned colder than glacier ice. Never bruise a man's ego.

Latoya was devastated. She was conflicted, dazed and confused. What should she have done? Had she gone along with his investment strategy, her money would have been compromised too.

Yes, but after a month of being alone she deemed that what she lost in JP, her future husband, was suddenly worth more than silver and gold. In the end, the pain, embarrassment and loneliness Latoya endured were far more damaging than the loss of a few thousand dollars. Latoya was truly distraught, and decided to confide in her mother and ask for relationship advice. After all, Mom had been married to Dad for over forty years.

The advice her mother gave her ultimately saved her relationship. She told Latoya about all the crazy ideas her father had tried and failed. This was a surprise to Latoya, who only knew her dad as the self-made millionaire who frequently switched companies. She was completely oblivious to his mishaps. When she spoke to her dad about it, he laughed and said, "You win some; you lose some." She immediately began to think about her mistake with JP and how miserably she failed the loyalty test.

Over dinner, her parents discussed the reality of marriage and the commitment it required to support one another for better or for worse. Latoya wondered why she had never confided in her parents before to guide in her relationships. She had no idea how clueless she was about the true purpose of marriage. She learned that selfishness has no place in a solid marriage.

Her mom told her about how she stood beside and supported her husband when he made a bad financial move in the real estate market despite his father-in-law's warning. In fact, they had to downgrade and reside in a rental property on the wrong side of town to make ends meet. She was furious, but she saw standing beside and supporting her husband as her duty.

She realized that her commitment was to her husband, not to material things.

Her dad confided that her mother's unconditional support and unfaltering loyalty prompted him to listen to her more and actively seek her input and support. He matured, became wiser and eventually consented to consult his father-in-law. Moreover, he worked his tail off to get back what they lost. Learning from his mistakes, he succeeded and eventually they lived the life of luxury as he rebuilt company after company with the backing and support of his beloved wife.

Latoya's dad admitted that with money came temptation and advances from younger but certainly not finer, women than his wife. "I never ventured outside our marriage because of the one thing your mom had over all of them: unconditional love and loyalty," her dad said with a smile that appeared a mile long and enough admiration to fill up their swimming pool in the back yard.

That conversation cleared up Latoya's confusion. She never understood why her dad rarely objected to her mom's lavish shopping excursions. What she misinterpreted as her dad's kindness and husbandly duty was instead a well-deserved reward for staying with him during his darkest days.

Latoya compared all men to her father and lacked respect when they were unable to demonstrate the financial acumen and generosity he exhibited. She now realized that her dad was imperfect, and her mother had to earn his superfluous doting. She immediately knew it was time to call JP to make restitution.

She thanked her parents, internalized their advice, and decided to raise the bar a notch. She was intent on making amends for her mistakes and reached out to a woman with whom she had frequently had conflict: JP's mother. It took three calls for his mom to accept her invitation for lunch. Latoya explained her mistake and asked for two things:

forgiveness and help. She loved JP with all her heart but could not get him to call her back. His mom accepted her apology and even apologized herself for not sharing words of wisdom before. They bonded over lunch and created a plan to get JP back.

Actually, it wasn't a plan. JP's mom called him and told him to listen to what Latoya had to say. Initially, he was appalled that Latoya had the gall to call his mother after the things she had to say about her; however, he was impressed that she thought enough of his mother to have lunch with her and, of all things, apologize. As angry and upset as he was, he couldn't resist the opportunity to hear the words, "I'm sorry." He asked Latoya when and where she wanted to meet, and she suggested the first of the three rental condominiums.

Latoya asked him to leave a key under the mat. JP obliged and got the surprise of a lifetime. When he entered, Latoya was dressed in black silk lingerie and four-inch heels that further accented her phenomenally sculpted thighs and calves. Her top, or lack thereof, revealed a healthy bosom and washboard stomach that perfectly bridged to her lace see-through panties, which left absolutely nothing to the imagination. She was preparing his favorite meal: Cornish hens, dressing, broccoli, and chocolate cake. That wasn't the biggest surprise, though. On the counter was a check for $5000 (double the investment he had put in) made out to JP.

JP was confused and unsure what to make of this sudden change in Latoya. They had not spoken in a month. He started to call his mom for putting Latoya up to this, but she stopped him in his tracks the way a woman is supposed to. She prepared his plate, serving him dessert first and straddled him while removing the cake icing off his lips, apologizing with her tongue. She told him about her conversations with her parents and his mom and said that if he would have her, she would gladly submit to him repeatedly for the rest of her life.

JP was almost sold, but he didn't like the feeling of being

bought for $5000. She laughed and explained that he would indeed forgive her because she loved him unconditionally and she looked forward to proving it. Later, she explained that the money was evidence of her trust in him and that it was also for hiring a company to manage the properties until the market improved.

Smiling, he remarked, "There you go trying to run things again."

She responded, "Baby, it's only a suggestion, and it's your mom's. Do with the money as you deem best for *us*. I trust you." This was music to JP's ears, and he couldn't resist one more bite of Latoya's chocolate cake.

At that point, JP fell back in love with Latoya. In a few weeks, she had her ring back on... with another carat in it. The property management company secured a three-year lease with a corporation that had recently opened up an office in the neighborhood and needed housing for interns. Latoya's suggestions worked perfectly.

JP and Latoya married nine months later, and soon they were expecting twins. Recognizing the talents of his beautiful wife, JP formed a company that she could run from home. He relinquished control over many aspects of his life because he trusted her, appreciated her devotion and submission and knew she trusted him.

Ladies, there is power in supportive submission. Any woman who is patient, loving and obedient enough to submit to God's order will make herself an invaluable asset to her man. With her, he is stronger and wiser. He is also indebted to her. By staying in her lane and focusing all her energy toward fortifying and supporting, instead of fighting, her man, she opens the door to all the control and love she could possibly desire.

Problems arise when the mindset going into relationships is wrong. If you doubt a man's ability to lead based on his lack of relationship with God, you should simply not enter into the union. Loneliness, age and desire for companionship sometimes force us to make decisions that go against our better judgment. When this happens, however, you must ask yourself, "Who am I following, and is the path in tune with what I believe?" If not, conflict will occur frequently as the luster of the relationship wanes, and you begin to openly defy his leadership and wander further and further away from harmony.

By contrast, women who make the unwise decision to battle men for head of household status are bound to fail miserably. It is a true lose-lose proposition. If she succeeds, the man will leave (physically, emotionally and/or sexually). If she fails and the couple argues over control, the friendship will surely suffer, thereby weakening the relationship.

Men must be allowed to lead. If not, two things will happen: (1) He will feel out of tune with man's divine nature, and (2) He will lose the respect of his partner. The intriguing dynamic about power struggles within relationships is that women actually expect and desire for men to use their power to demonstrate why they should be supportively submissive to them.

Once men prove themselves strong enough and worthy, women will usually submit and harmony can begin. As wives are supposed to submit to their husbands, husbands are also required to love their wives as God loved the church. When the two focus on taking care of the other's needs first then true love can blossom and flourish.

Sometimes, however, women can be too strong for their own good! They say they don't need or respect a man, and genuinely feel that their worldly accomplishments give them license to "run the household." This type of woman is almost always single or in conflict with strong men. The problem is that, to men, this sounds like you want to be the man. How can any healthy relationship between a man and a woman have two men? Besides, a woman who is INDEPENDENT has no use for a man anyway.

Men like strong, educated, talented women who also know how to be soft, pretty and gentle at home. No man likes a woman who nags, barks in his face, openly challenges his authority or uses her worldly power to manipulate or dominate him. When this occurs, emotionally and physically charged exchanges become more common. Men are simply ill equipped to process or accept such behavior because it absolutely undermines the core of their being.

Men are leaders by nature and all desire to lead. As witnessed in the play of young boys, every male battles to be King of the Hill, and their play always reflects power struggles. Men are used to competing with other males and respect the natural order when they either win or lose in "battle" with one another. Men are rarely jealous of who is picked to be captain of the team if he has demonstrated superior ability. This also explains why males are able to disagree and quickly reconcile. Quite simply, if you beat me up, you deserve my respect. Once respect is restored, friendship can commence.

But what are men to do with women who desire, communicate, and behave like men? How should they respond with this very real threat to rule and control him? The answers are plentiful, and none are healthy (abuse, disengagement, extra-marital affairs). My advice to my brethren is the same as for the sisters. If a woman does not agree with the divine order of gender roles, choose not to enter into the relationship. Ultimately, conflict will arise as you fight to the death (of the relationship) to assume what you believe you are both entitled to.

It is imperative that you intimately understand man's innate desire to be head of household, protector and provider for the family. These roles are necessary to maintain his sensitive but important ego. The key to harmony is to embrace men's desire to lead, stay in your lane, and welcome your position as the perfect complement or helper to fortify them. Women and men are the same since both share the same rib, but they have vastly different roles within the relationship. Man fortifies the woman and woman fortifies the man. This is why we long to feel completed by one another and strongly desire harmonious relationships.

So what is the solution? I think it is simple when both parties realize that they are individually stronger as a unit. To become a fortified unit, you must accept your role and stay in your lane; however, according to God's divine order, the man should assume the lead, while the woman stands by his side in support. Remember that most married men defer to their wives anyway because she is usually the best COO (Chief Operating Officer) or manager of the house. A smart wife will verbally say that her husband is in charge but everyone knows (including her husband) who really gives the orders. The funny thing is that the large majority of husbands *prefer* this arrangement. Men are used to completing "honey-do" lists, asking for permission to have a Super Bowl parties and convincing the children to straighten up before mom (the boss we all have to answer to) gets home.

If you still find yourself struggling with the word submission then read the application section because, chances are, you have yet to experience its true power and seeing is believing.

Application Section

In the introduction, I indicated that this was a book specifically written for women who wanted to get married or stay married. It was not written for bitter women. However, it was brought to my attention that men are sometimes legitimate causes of temporary feelings of bitterness. I concur and want to help so I will focus this application section on anyone having bitter feelings about submission because an ex-boyfriend, abusive or absent father did not value the beautiful woman that God created you to be.

The first question that you must truthfully ask yourself is, DO YOU WANT A MAN? For some of you, that answer is No and that is okay. However, you must stop complaining about being single, embrace it as a choice and wear it with a smile. For the rest of you who do seek love, commitment and marriage despite past pain, good for you! You have decided to avoid playing the game of self-protection and trust God to provide you with clearer judgment on choice of partners. After all, it would be tragic to allow pride, unresolved feelings of resentment (however legitimate they may be) and/or a basic lack of understanding of men to ruin your chances at marriage.

It never ceases to amaze me just how different women act once they listen, observe, learn and truly understand men. They are easy to spot and usually marry quickly because they know how to handle men. Men are very strange fruit but can actually be rather simple once you understand their needs.

1) Men need to be heard

2) Men need to *feel* in control

3) Men fear inadequacy

In my experience, women who understand these basic principles date with the upper hand. Have you ever asked yourself why so many women have no problem with being submissive to their husbands? Certainly, they are strong, intelligent and very capable women, right? Why would they willingly submit and give up power to a man? Do they really need to "dumb down", be quiet and follow the leader just to make a man happy? The answer is yes and no. The key to *wanting* to submit is realizing the intended definition of the word and enjoying its benefits.

When we think of submission, we automatically think about someone ruling or dominating us. Our nature (men and women) is to resist oppression and free ourselves. Additionally, with the history of sexism in this world it certainly makes sense not to allow men to "rule" you. However, too many people confuse oppression and submission. The original definition of submission is the "act of referring to a third party for judgment or decision". Another definition is "humble submission."

When you think about God, you certainly have no problems submitting to HIS will. Men have no problems submitting to God either, if they are a believer. After all, who really has control in this world above God? So much anxiety, stress and doubt can be released once you realize that the Creator is in control and to allow God to lead your life. So, think about it differently. Instead of submitting to your man, who is fallible, decide to submit to the God in your man.

Quite naturally, one might ask, "Why can't we both be equal then and equally submit to God instead of using man as the intermediary"? Excellent question and let me try to explain. MEN NEED TO LEAD. A man who does not lead does not feel like a man. You may prefer to lead because you possess advanced leadership abilities, but your man's ego and your relationship will suffer. He will begin to slack which ultimately leads you to being displeased because you realize that you need him to lead to respect him as a man.

Here's where your role as a wo-man (notice that man is in your title) becomes so integral. You are a helper and it's obvious that men need a lot of help these days. Quite simply, you make men better leaders. In fact, you make men better EVERYTHING (healthier, smarter, richer, wiser, calmer, more patient, more responsible, more focused, more balanced, better godfathers, mentors, teachers, neighbors, church servants, etc.). Beautiful ladies, don't be fooled by crazy guys with inferiority complexes and sexist attitudes. You were not created to simply serve, be oppressed, shut up and be quiet. You were created because men NEED your help. The problem is that we hate asking for it because it clashes with our ego. Our primary fear is inadequacy and we go throw extraordinary means to hide it and over-compensate for it at all costs.

Let me explain some basic gender differences. Men do not fear being homeless. Women do. Women typically fear being hurt, lonely, disconnected from friends and being unable to provide the things necessary for happiness. Men, on the other hand, can handle homelessness. We feel like we can protect ourselves, hold our own, cut our expenses and power up. Once we power up, we can then reconnect with friends and family and buy our man toys (electronics, gadgets, motorcycles, cars, etc.).

What men fear, which is in direct contrast to women, is other people finding out that we are homeless. This exposes our inadequacy to the entire world and we would rather die. Women, on the other hand, will call a friend for emotional support and discuss every tragic detail of how she became homeless. Men will never tell and will likely never speak to you again if you tell anyone. We feel like we can always heal ourselves. That is exactly why we struggle with depression, alcohol, drug abuse, gambling, sex addictions, etc.; all because we hate asking for help. It makes us feel weak, inadequate and feminine (an insult to a man).

Did you know that the research indicates that married men are wealthier, happier, healthier and enjoy higher life expectancy than men who are unmarried? Do you think that is by sheer coincidence? Absolutely not! Men need women to make them stronger in every aspect of their lives. In fact, men frequently credit their "better half" for encouraging them, fortifying them and making them the man they are today. Wow, that's sounds an awful lot like mom's influence doesn't it? Men do need you. That's why the smart ones are wise enough to court you and put a ring on your finger to make you exclusive. All we basically need you to do is to make us *feel* like we are in control.

Here is a mental treat ladies and a truth that men will privately concede:

"Men don't always want to be in control, we just want you to say that we are."

I cannot believe I just told you that but, oh well, it's the truth. We just like to FEEL like we are in control. This is why women who truly understand men are so effective and often married. They know that men need help but won't ask for it. So being the smart, talented and confident helper and nurturer that you are, you help us by becoming the world's smartest psychologist. You manage to help us while magically convincing us that it was our idea all along. That way, we are helping ourselves. Wow, you are smart and thank God you are in our lives.

Here's the funny thing. Men are not stupid. We know our wives are playing head games with us. We know it was your idea that we build a website, work smarter versus harder, eat better, etc. but you cared enough about our need to feel adequate and powerful that you stroked our egos anyway.

This, ladies, is a labor of love and the reason why men marry. They know beyond a shadow of a doubt that any woman who respects his power while making him stronger is an asset for life. Men are not in the business of losing assets and only drop you when you become a liability (an ego killer). They need you to turn Clark Kent into Superman not vice versa.

Men are warriors and heal quickly in capable hands. We can go from loser to winner in a short period of time with the right amount of love. Secretly, most high profile performers and athletes will admit that their wives are their psychologist and keep their heads right. Teams actually encourage men to marry to keep their athletes out of the streets and to ensure that daily empowerment is occurring when he hits a rough performance stretch. In appreciation, men spend the majority of their time and money to make their wives happy, secure and satisfied.

Okay, enough talk. Let's practice! I'm going to give you some scenarios and then see if you give the correct response. Are you ready to make an A? Need I remind you that men love smart women? Let's see who rises to the top of the class. The Doc is in, let the test begin.

1) Your man is obviously lost and won't ask directions. What should you say or do to ensure that you get to your destination on time?

A) Tell him the directions.
B) Remain quiet and allow him to find it on his own.
C) Offer to drive.
D) Tell him how great he is with directions and ask him which way to go.

If you answered "D" you are correct! Let me explain why so that you don't make this mistake with your man. If you tell him the directions before he asks you, he will think that you are trying to be in charge or "be the man" and will resist. In fact, he may refuse to ask for directions despite being late to prove to you (and to himself) that he is the man in the relationship.

If you remain quiet then he will wonder around aimlessly because he is too embarrassed to ask for directions. Your silence implies that you trust him to find it and he will melt under the expectation if his directional skills are poor.

If you offer to drive, then you have completely emasculated him. If he allows you to drive because he is lost then you have broken this man's spirit and he is useless. However, if you stroke his ego by telling him that you know he can find it because he always does then you will be on time and have an appreciative boyfriend and future husband by your side. See, once you affirm his manhood, he is now able to ask you to navigate him to the proper destination. He is the captain but you are the navigator. Alone, he drives all day and night but with you he can gets to the same destinations in half the time.

2) Your man has lost his job and won't communicate with you. He appears to be shutting down while the bills pile up. What should you do?

A) Help him to find a job
B) Withhold sex until he finds a job to encourage him
C) Express your views about a man's role; to work
D) Triple up physical intimacy and sex (if married)

If you answered "A," you are incorrect again. Men never need help due to pride. We are conditioned to be the provider, protector and leader of the relationship and family. How can a truly capable leader *need* help from his woman? His pride won't allow him to accept your help because it makes him feel weak. He might get the job but lose his manhood and you don't want to deal with that.

If you answered B, you are incorrect as well. Withholding sex to teach him a lesson or inspire him will backfire 100% of the time. It will only make him feel worse and introduce the idea that you only love him because he has money, job or influence. You are practically begging him to have an affair when you do this.

If you answered C then you are wrong too. The last thing that a man who has lost his job wants to do is to talk about losing his job. Additionally, he does not want a lecture or to hear your thoughts and feelings about him not being a man because he doesn't work.

However, if you answered D, you are on a roll. Men are like babies and need physical affection when wounded. Men tie their egos around their jobs. Thus, losing a job is devastating to a man because his ego is hurt. However, if you stroke that huge ego of his and psychologically empower him by telling him that you believe in him, he will work from sun up to sun down to impress you with his new job. Good job, you just stroked your man to a better paying job! Now, you can go out to eat more.

3) Your man walks in the house from work and doesn't speak. He starts his routine of watching television, reading the newspaper, showering, etc. What do you do to get him to speak without arguing?

A) Ask him why he's not speaking?
B) Tell him it's rude to come in the house without speaking.
C) Ignore him back.
D) Give him a back massage.

If you answered "A" again, you should be ashamed of yourself. You should know that if he didn't speak when he entered that he was unlikely to speak upon query.

If you answered "B," then you are human but headed for an argument. Men hate arguing all the time and especially after a long day's work. Men need to unwind for a few minutes when they get home to transition into husband and father mode. You are right that he should greet you when he comes home but confronting him verbally will likely lead to him secluding himself or even leaving the house. It's not that he doesn't love you but he needs to be trained to greet you and then enjoy peace of mind after a crazy day on the job.

If you answered "C," then you are enabling inappropriate behavior. After all, you worked hard all day too and still managed to prepare a hot, home cooked meal for the family. Additionally, this pattern will likely continue because he may not even realize that he did anything wrong. After all, you didn't say anything to him about it. Your feelings are important and will likely bubble over as the night goes on. When you do finally mention to him, he'll swear that you are making it up because you failed to say anything to him earlier.

For those of you who answered "D," I am thoroughly impressed! On the surface, this answer appears crazy because it looks like you are rewarding bad behavior. However, if you understand men then you know that they respond to touch far better than words. In fact, studies reflect that men require two to three times of physical affection than women to feel loved. Women talk to connect while men need to connect to talk.

Also, remember that you catch more bees with honey, especially after a long day. As soon as you begin giving him a back massage, he is likely to thank you and apologize for not greeting his queen. Don't be surprised if he grabs your hands and pulls you onto his lap and asks about your day. Now that sounds like an invitation for extra dessert.

4) Initially, you cannot open a jar. However, if you exert a little muscle, you are likely to find that you can open it yourself. Should you open it or ask your man to help?

Please tell me that you let that man open the jar! Men need to feel needed. This is why men dislike "independent" women because they render his services useless. Boys grow up dreaming about being superheroes so that they can save the world and rescue damsels in distress. Thus, he needs to open jars, cans, and fix things to realize that dream. You have no idea how much opening that jar makes a man feel like King Kong. It also lowers his insecurities because it serves as proof that you do need him.

5) You hear a strange noise at home. What should you do if your man is home? What should you do if he is not at home or doesn't live with you?

Let me start by saying that I am not a proponent of playing games but I do endorse the power of stroking a man's ego. In order to satisfy a man's innate desire to feel adequate, he needs to feel needed by you. The problem is that he will rarely, if ever, communicate that need due to his pride. This is just something that you should already know as a woman. Allowing a man to protect and keep you safe is like giving him a trophy for "World's Greatest Man."

The next time you hear a strange noise at home, which could be anytime (smile), jump up like you are scared and ask your husband to check it out. He may say that he didn't hear anything but insist that he check it out because you can't rest until he does. Look into his eyes like he is Superman and clasp onto his biceps and softly ask him to check it out. He'll get up, check it out and report back that everything is fine. When he reenters the bedroom, hug him and apologize for being a "fraidy-cat". Chances are that he won't need your apology because you've done him a big favor; you made him feel needed and like a Roman gladiator.

Snuggle up next to him and whisper in his ear, "Baby, I feel so much safer around you," and kiss him on the cheek. He may not show it due to his warrior code but trust that he is smiling from ear to ear when he turns over. Since you are married already, I would begin to caress him provocatively and enjoy the response. After all, don't damsels in distress always reward the hero?

What about you lovely ladies who are yet to be married? Here's what you do. Make sure that it's not too late but late enough for you to be reasonably be afraid. Call your man and tell him that your alarm went off or that you heard a strange noise. Ask him if he would come over for a few minutes and check it out. Most men will say yes because, again, this makes them feel needed.

When he arrives and discovers that all is safe, genuinely hug him for traveling all the way across town to check on you. Kiss him, squeeze him tight and tell him, "Baby, I feel so safe in your arms." If he does not live close, offer the couch for him to sleep on so he doesn't have to drive home so late and then fix him some warm dessert (not you silly-save that for marriage). It won't be extra work for you since you already have a warm apple pie in the oven anyway. Hey, don't laugh. You are playing for keeps right?

If you plan it well, then you will call him on Friday night and he won't have to work on Saturday. Wake up early, hand him some toiletries, a towel and a wash cloth so he can clean up. While he is washing up, start preparing the breakfast of his life- maybe an omelet, pancakes, Eggs Benedict, steak or salmon with eggs, fish and grits, homemade biscuits with fresh squeezed orange juice or pomegranate blueberry juice (my favorite).

After breakfast, thank him for coming over so late and send some of your biscuits home with him to eat later. Ladies, don't get seduced and lose your discipline by allowing him to bed you or stay over all day Saturday. Remember to give him only chip at a time to keep him hungry and coming back for more. I guarantee you that if you do this correctly, he won't care if you get a million dollar raise at work because of how well you treat him. Besides, money can't keep you warm, safe and protected at night. Is that your alarm going off?

6) What should you do if you make more money than your man and you are getting signs that he is becoming envious?

This is a very relevant question because chances are that both of your incomes will fluctuate over time. Men desire to be the provider to satisfy their need to feel adequate and the leader of the household. If any unexpected expense arises, he wants to be able to tell you not to worry about it because you are with him and that he'll "take care of it". However, this is not always possible, especially in a recession.

It's important that you know that men base a large part of their ego on their job title and performance. Thus, if they are struggling at work and to provide at home then unhappiness is sure to follow. Thus, it is important to be prepared to spring into action to avoid him acting out in a manner that damages the marriage.

There are two groups of men who are able to handle their woman making more money. The first group are men who have a very strong relationship with the Lord and don't tie their ego around only money and/or are very confident about their ability to out-earn you over time. The second group of men are the HUSBANDS who lucky enough to be married to you (smile). You are a Ring Formula Woman and are trained for such situations. You realize that your profession and your role as his wife are distinctly different and adjust accordingly.

At work, if someone is not producing at work then you will lead them (male or female) to produce higher results or find another job. However, at home, you kiss your husband, take his briefcase and fix him something to eat when he arrives. This may sound crazy to you but I invite you to ask powerful women who remain married how they treat their husbands. After all, it is far easier to replace a job than a husband.

Make sure that you always make a man feel like a man by behaving like a lady. When planning vacations, allow him to make the final call on how much to spend, even if you have the extra money. I know you like to stay in nice places but remember that you are playing for keeps. Once he sees that you are willing to respect his power, he will likely soften to allow for an upgrade or two. After all, your vacation should not be spent at the Budget Inn three miles off the beach.

Give him time, reassure him that he is your King and tell him that you know what kind of provider he is. Tell him that you look forward to him whisking you away to Paris someday as his business and dreams grow and that you would rather have him than money any day. Tell him that relationships/marriages are about partnerships and that you are both fortunate to have the means to afford a vacation. Also, make sure you tell him that you enjoy getting his back and do not wish to lead. That's right, verbalize his issue and solve it in the same sentence.

For really sensitive men, make sure you get cash and allow him to pay for all meals, expenses, etc when you go on vacation. If you must use credit then balance transfer the money to his account so that he can pay the bills. A man must feel and be treated like the man at all times to be happy. You can enjoy the finest food and wine in the world, back dropped by a picturesque view of the ocean just to have it ruined when the server hands him the bill and he has to pass it to you. I mean really, who's securing who? Please understand how hard this is for men and take the necessary steps to respect his position. Chances are that, over time, his income may surpass yours and you'll be enjoying the view of the Eiffel Tower in Paris as a reward for staying in your lane when he couldn't afford such trips.

7) A man ask you out on a date and hands you the bill or request that you to split it. What should you do?

I used to have a preset plan to pay for the first few meals and then allow my date to pay for the fifth. I simply wanted to see if she was willing to share her income with me as a trust exercise. This plan worked well until I met my current significant other. After our fifth date, I slid the bill to her only to be met with the meanest look I've ever seen. I still remember her exact words, "Alduan, I am traditional woman who does not pay for meals. Now, occasionally I may treat you as my man but it's not something that I make common practice."

"Well, have you ever thought that men like to be treated too from time to time?" I recanted. "Absolutely baby, that's why I cook for you all the time. How many times have you eaten over my house- four times?" "That's about right," I responded with a smirk. "Well alright then," she responded and slid the bill back across the table. When she saw that I still did not comprehend she explained, "Alduan, when you cook for someone it costs money. You've had lobster, salmon, crab claws, shrimp, and scallops- all fresh too- not to mention dessert, wine, and that crazy Pomegranate Blueberry juice you like..." I stopped her midsentence because I got the point, "Waiter, here's the check," as I slid *my* debit card inside. My significant other had convinced me that I liked the traditional approach much more than the modern one, besides those crab claws were to die for!

I encourage each one of you to use this strategy or some deviation that works for you as a couple. Find ways to make each other feel worthy while standing your ground on having your needs met. One-sided love affairs never work so communicate to make sure that you are both happy and sufficiently courting one another.

If a man does not want to pay for your meal, especially after *he* invited you out (which is the only way you two would go to dinner anyway) then he is not worth the paper napkin from the cheap restaurant he likely picked out. Move on the next one and treat him like a King. He's likely a real man and will probably order you a second helping for you to eat at lunch tomorrow. Can you say, Mr. Big!

Summary of Wise Tips

Albert Einstein was quoted as saying the following about his wife on their fiftieth wedding anniversary:

When we first got married, we made a pact. It was this: In our life together, it was decided I would make all the big decisions and my wife would make all of the little decisions. For fifty years, we have held true to that agreement. I believe that is the reason for the success of our marriage. However, the strange thing is that in fifty years, there hasn't been one big decision.

Ring Formula Tip # 1

Be dumb like a fox because men *love* foxes!

Ring Formula Tip # 2

When you allow a man to feel powerful, you evoke his will to protect you and give you the world.

Ring Formula Tip # 3

When you cater to a man's ego in a soft way, he doesn't try to get power in an aggressive way.

Ring Formula Tip # 4

When a woman acts as if she can do anything a man can do, she gets stuck doing everything while the man does nothing.

Ring Formula Tip # 5

Men don't respond to words. Instead, they respond to contact or lack thereof.

Ring Formula Tip # 6

When you are always upbeat and happy and he feels always free to go, he feels lucky and comes home early.

Ring Formula Tip # 7

Be the navigator not the driver.

Ring Formula Tip # 8

If you discount yourself from the start then he will never see you for your full value.

Ring Formula Tip # 9

Even if men ask for it, they rarely respect anything (or anyone) that comes too easily. Easy come, easy go.

Ring Formula Tip # 10

Men need you to be secure in who you are so you can make them secure in who they are.

Ring Formula Tip # 11

A praying woman is a far more powerful woman than a screaming one.

Ring Formula Tip # 12

Men desire a helpmate not help because it implies weakness. Instead, ask how you can "assist".

Ring Formula Tip # 13

ALL men desire for the woman to be the C.O.O (Chief Operating Officer) of the house.

Formula FIVE

GREAT SEX IS NOT ENOUGH
MEN MARRY FRIENDS NOT FREAKS

"Would you ever invest in a car without first looking under the hood?" The psychology of men is complex and laden with issues that are often difficult to navigate. As a woman seeking a meaningful, long-lasting relationship, it behooves you to learn how to check under the hood to find which set of issues you can and cannot deal with at the onset of the relationship. Men can be difficult to understand because of different communication styles; what appears on the surface to be a burning desire may be the exact opposite on a deeper level. Deciphering what men really want can be quite confusing and frustrating if you are not in tune with what men really need but neglect to communicate.

Three groups of people enjoy significant success in finding out what goes on in the minds of men: parents, best friends and psychologists. Chances are that neither family members nor his boys are going to spill the beans, so I guess that leaves you with me—the psychologist. Lucky for you, this psychologist is willing to share the winning recipe necessary to encourage that special man to reveal his insecurities, fears, and true desires to you at the beginning of your relationship so you can decide whether he is your MR. RIGHT.

A growing bastion of women are ascribing to the F.S.L. philosophy for making men happy. F.S.L. stands for Feed him,

Sex him, and Let him have his way. The process can also be described as the "fizzle syndrome" because, given time, that is exactly what will happen to your relationship.

While men all over the world are nodding their heads in agreement because, on the surface, this is what they want, most will agree that a greater engagement is necessary to enter into a monogamous relationship and marriage. FSL represents only the most basic of carnal needs and merely fulfilling them will not get you any closer to wife status. In fact, only meeting them will undoubtedly get you further away.

On a deeper level, men truly desire another type of F.S.L., which stands for Friendship, Support, and Loyalty. For women, this represents the right way to "Find some Serious Loving." Friendship is more valuable than food. Support is more enduring than great sex and your man appreciates loyalty far more than he wants to be left alone.

What men look for in a wife are virtues that are more consistent with friendship (trustworthiness, loyalty, dedication, respect, willingness to listen, understanding, supportiveness, a good sense of humor, and compassion). Yes, men do want wives who are curvaceous, pretty and great in bed, but inner beauty is far more important and enduring when seeking a soul mate. Men realize that all the superficial beauty and wonderful sex in the world won't overcome the trials that come with five, ten or twenty years of marriage.

Despite what you may see with your own eyes regarding society's insistent focus on superficial beauty, real men truly seek and desire friendship, albeit they have odd ways of communicating that. Within men, there resides an ever-raging conflict between the basic drive state for food, sex and independence and the deeper need for genuine friendship and quality companionship. Lack of self-discipline causes men to be preoccupied with the fulfillment of sexual pleasure and a need for unbridled freedom. Men make colossal mistakes when they cannot bring this drive under control.

Just look at how many men from heads of state to church elders are brought down to their knees because of lack of self-discipline. Women who recognize men's inner turmoil and opt to stand on higher ground by resisting physical advances and late-night phone calls will earn lasting respect and enjoy staying power.

So what are you supposed to do when your man outright demands sex and independence? This is where YOUR self-discipline takes over. Simply refuse to compromise your morals, and opt to develop friendship, support and loyalty instead. Although men certainly will throw some form of temper tantrums after being turned down for sex, ultimately they respect you and work hard to earn your companionship.

The formula for courting MR. RIGHT towards the altar is to commit to becoming friends before lovers, much like the character played by Halle Berry in the movie *Boomerang* in her pursuit of Eddie Murphy. Learn to separate sex and love into two distinct boxes. Shun the FSL basic instinct philosophy and replace it with meeting his deeper, emotional needs to promote a long-lasting relationship. Take control and place yourself only in the box labeled "Friend and Biggest Supporter." The path to wife status resides there.

Finding out what men really want in a wife is synonymous to shopping at the mall. If you base all your decisions on strolling down the corridor and simply window-shopping, you will miss the true value inside the stores. You have to be knowledgeable enough to make sure you aren't fooled. In the display window, men may display for shoppers that "Great Sex Leads to Marriage," but nothing could be further from the truth. In fact, giving in to a man's desire for sex too early is an absolute relationship killer.

Therefore, it is important to know the difference between what men want right now (e.g., Saturday night) versus what they desire long-term (marriage) because they are distinctly different. On the surface, to the untrained ear, the two sound and feel the same. You have to be patient and discerning to recognize the difference. Doing so can save you heartache, pain and time.

Despite common sense, many well-meaning women err by mentioning or having sex too soon into the relationship. They either bought into the false advertising or responded to the pressures of the market place. Women feel that in the heat of the battle, if they don't *"give it up"* someone else will. They fail to realize that what their intended partner really wants is friendship, even though he may have asked for sex.

They focus on the immediacy of the superficial instead of patiently building something that will last. As a result, they feel the pain of rejection and feelings of disloyalty when the relationship does not work out because their man has no desire to settle down...at least with them.

These women look up one day and sadly realize that they have invested years trying to cultivate a long-term relationship only to learn that they put themselves in the "We Can Have Sex but Not Marriage" box. Upon realizing their mistake and demanding to switch boxes, their man has difficulty accepting that, and the relationship ends. Men have tremendous difficulty upgrading a woman's status from sex partner to wife when the initial relationship was largely built on sex.

Men will be brutally honest after the fact and state the obvious: "You should have never had sex with me if that's what you wanted." In the minds of men, psychologically it really is too late. Utterly devastated, the woman reflects on all the good men she ignored and time she wasted focusing on a man who never intended to commit to her after the first sexual encounter.

The definition of insanity is "doing the same thing you've always done while expecting different results." Simply relying on meeting a man's basic needs will surely doom you to a lifetime of insanity as you navigate through the revolving door of dead-end relationships. In fact, trying to grow a relationship on sex alone can be a slippery slope. If you over rely on it or use it too much, you will box yourself up so tight you will rob yourself of ever being regarded as marriage material.

Courting men can be futile and fruitless without the right approach. Just ask Jasmine.

Jasmine was young, hot, and naïve. A Houston native, Jasmine ate well, and her body displayed it in all the right places. Despite only being 5'3", Jasmine was stacked. What she lacked in height she more than made up for in hips, thighs, and chest.

Her skin was bronze, and she could have been compared with an Elite Fashion Fair model. She sauntered down the avenue as if she were on the catwalk, swinging her red and white trimmed Fendi spy bag, masquerading in quarter-high Gucci boots that accented her shapely calves and rimming her delicate features with Channel shades. Her short-cropped, layered hairstyle, French-manicured nails, and small wrist draped with a signature diamond-studded tennis bracelet reflected her Diva mentality.

Feisty and opinionated, Jasmine never met attention she didn't like. However, at twenty-six, she was growing tired of the dating scene and was ready to settle down.

Outwardly flirtatious and bold with an adventurous nature, she inwardly desired a man who would balance her spirit and make her want to submit, calm down, and begin a family. As she mentally prepared to "lock down" a good husband for herself, she surveyed her body and smiled. She knew that every man has a sweet tooth and she definitely qualified as eye candy.

Jasmine's philosophy was, "If you have it, flaunt it" and that's exactly what she did. Jasmine got attention everywhere she went. She couldn't go the grocery store or the cleaners without being propositioned for dates, music videos and movies. Getting attention from men was far from her problem; maintaining it was.

Jasmine averaged two to three dates per week and had more than enough options from which to choose. The first date was frequently a positive experience because of her upbeat personality and seductive energy. She easily secured second and third dates that would quickly evolve into relationship status. She was incessantly hopeful that things would steadily progress into a monogamous commitment and eventual marriage; however, like clockwork, she would experience a sudden and unwanted downward spiral in her relationships, generally after submitting to sex.

Jasmine loved having sex and made it no secret that she needed to see if a man could satisfy her before she could commit to him for life; however, she was cautious not to send the wrong message to men and experimented with delaying intimacy for a few months into the relationship. No matter what she tried, the outcome was always the same; her date would immediately lose interest and eventually stop calling. Jasmine was confused because the sex was great; her partners confirmed it! In her mind, there was no way SEX could be the real culprit.

Jasmine was stressed and getting extremely worried. She began to feel as if she were participating in a soul train line instead of finding a soul mate. To help her sort out her dilemma, a friend suggested that she seek a professional relationship coach.

Determined to solve the mystery of the series of fleeting relationships, she wasted no time in setting up an appointment. She quickly connected with Dr. T., a very personable female psychologist. Dr. T. wasted no time in assessing all the possible reasons for Jasmine's revolving door of eligible bachelors.

The first order of business was to explore Jasmine's ideas

about the best way to attract and maintain the attention of men. Without much delving, it became obvious that Jasmine's focus was on her superficial qualities.

"I'm pretty, in great shape, and dress to impress," she bragged.

Jasmine was very proud of her physical attributes and the attention they garnered. She had been making men drool for years and was addicted to the attention. In fact, she craved it because it served as frequent validation that she was highly desirable.

Jasmine revealed that she enjoyed attending happy hours and nightclubs. "That's my element," she plugged. She truly loved being the life of the party and never heard a song to which she could not and would not dance. Having studied dance for eleven years as a teenager and young adult, Jasmine had a passion and talent for dance. She always suggested that dancing be included when dating. After all, her partner needed to be able to cut a rug to get and keep her attention.

Jasmine had a theory that she could tell a lot about a man's sexual prowess from how well he danced. She explained how dancing made her feel "alive, powerful and in control."

Dr. T. found the combination of dancing, power and control very intriguing. She encouraged Jasmine to explore this association on numerous occasions, but Jasmine struggled to make sense of it. After minutes of reflection all she could manage to say was, "You'd have to see it to understand it because I can't explain it."

The look in Jasmine's eyes and sudden shift in body language sparked her coach's curiosity. Being a woman herself, Dr. T. had a good idea of what she meant but did not want to rush to judgment. She shook her head wondering, "Does this girl understand what she's doing?"

Dr. T. had no idea that she would have an opportunity to see firsthand only a few weeks later. Within the black professional community, the social networking scene can be too small for anonymity at times. This was clearly the case when Dr. T and Jasmine separately received and accepted an e-vite to the premiere of a professional networking happy hour.

Within minutes of arriving at the event, Jasmine and Dr. T. were face-to-face, both surprised and caught off guard. They bumped into one another in the bathroom and found themselves side by side perfecting their makeup in the mirror. Excited that the power dynamics had suddenly changed, Jasmine couldn't resist giving Dr. T. some make-up suggestions by commenting, "MAC doesn't make your lips peel as much."

She wasn't coy, but playfully invited Dr. T. to observe and learn.

Dr. T. was a little uncomfortable with seeing her client in a social setting but since Jasmine obviously welcomed it, she decided to stay and observe her client's behavior. Before the majority of the crowd could arrive, Jasmine had already snatched up a handsome young man and was on the dance floor. It only took Dr. T. five minutes to recognize the problem and associate Jasmine's preoccupation with dancing, control and power.

Jasmine had everyone on the dance floor mesmerized as she moved effortlessly around the floor song after song. Her years of professional dance experience showed and made her the source of attention for all onlookers. Most intriguing was not *how* she danced, but the look in her eyes *while* she danced.

People could feel her vibe from across the room and it certainly didn't scream "long-term companionship." Instead, it said just the opposite: "Look at me. I need attention." It didn't take Dr. T. long to witness how clueless Jasmine really was.

"And to think she has the nerve to give *me* advice," Dr. T. diagnosed as she continued to observe her client's antics.

After seven songs, a tired scene, and no distraction from Jasmine's tribute to *Soul Train*, Dr. T. called it an evening. She had an overwhelming need to wash her hands and seek some true relaxation. After all, she needed to get a good night's sleep, so she could get an early start on helping this poor girl in the morning.

When they met for their coaching session the following day, Dr. T. inquired if Jasmine was aware of the message she sent at the club.

"Oh, you liked that, Doc? I told you that was my element, girl," Jasmine bragged.

Taken aback by Jasmine's newly found sense of familiarity, Dr. T. instructed her to "Please call me Dr. T." She prepped Jasmine with, "I'm not sure you want to hear this, but it will be for your benefit in the end."

"I know, I know," Jasmine infused. "I'm saying look at me; I'm sexy."

"Oh, you're aware?" Dr T. replied with a look of surprise.

"Sure, I like the attention. In a way, I guess I need it."

"That's obvious," Dr. T. chimed in.

Offended, Jasmine shot back, "Excuse me? Maybe you should loosen up a little and try it for yourself. You might catch a man."

Not one to back down, Dr. T. asked her in a professional manner, "How well is that working for you, Jasmine?"

Jasmine's sarcasm and overly inflated sense of self was immediately put to rest. After mutual apologies, they eventually settled back into the issue at hand -- Jasmine's relationship problems.

Dr. T. led Jasmine on an exploration of what happens after she meets a potential suitor. Dinner, movies and concerts were the normal course of events. Jasmine disclosed that she had a tendency to become smitten quickly and often wondered if each date was her eventual soul mate. Jasmine was certainly not one to pump the brakes and couldn't wait for an exclusive, loving and committed relationship to take off quickly.

Once involved in a new relationship, Jasmine made sure to refuse all sexual advances despite really being attracted to all of her dates. She explained that she did not want them to confuse her dancing with a lack of class or being easy. In fact, she considered herself rather conservative regarding marriage, preferring more traditional gender roles; however, she was blunt in stating, "Hey, a girl does have her needs, though."

She explained that when the time was right and she deemed the relationship secure, she would "go with the flow and let whatever happens, happen." Her relationships, however, quickly turned negative, and the budding chemistry would come to a screeching halt after sex. Instead of staying to talk or cuddle, her dates dressed quickly and ran for the hills. They ran the game that "everything is cool, but I'm late for work," but she knew better. They would still call but always late at night, avoiding another daylight date.

It was the same old thing repeatedly. She felt like a slave to the endless cycle of meeting and greeting, becoming intimate and being the unwanted costar in every brother's rendition of Terri McMillan's, *Disappearing Acts*. Jasmine reluctantly admitted that each time she would swallow her pride and inquire, "What am I doing wrong?" with tears of self-pity welling up inside her. She got many one-liners but never felt she got an honest answer.

Dr. T. listened intently, professionally comforting Jasmine as best she could, encouraging her to take as long as she needed to have a healthy cry. She was finally able to comfort

Jasmine by convincing her that she had discerned both the problem and the answer. She assured Jasmine that she could gain control over her love life and enjoy the long-term relationship she so desperately sought if she was willing to make a minor shift in mindset.

Dr. T. gave Jasmine a crash course in the psychology of men. She advised her that she absolutely, positively needed to retire the *Soul Train* dance routine if she intended to secure a relationship that was comprised of more than great but fleeting sex. Next, she challenged Jasmine to accept the fact that she used men's preoccupation with sex as a crutch. Jasmine heard but did not listen.

Obstinately, Jasmine objected. "That's not true. I told you that I set boundaries, make these fools wait and you never see me in hoochie-wear. I'm always clothed from head to toe."

Dr. T. explained, "Jasmine, first impressions frame everything and perception dictates reality. The men could care less how you dress after the fact. They are only focused on disrobing that sexy vixen with whom they first danced. Jasmine, men are visual creatures and slaves to their sex drive."

"I know that; tell me something I don't already know," Jasmine snapped. "So I use sex appeal to attract men. What woman doesn't?"

"The ones who can offer a man more than just good sex," Dr. T. answered, as she looked Jasmine squarely in the eye.

Hurt, surprised at Dr. T's boldness, and shamelessly prideful, Jasmine struck back, "OK, you've gone too far. Where is *your* man, Doc? I didn't see a single man approach you last night, and you have the nerve to give me tips. You've let that Ph.D. go to your head. With me, Dr. T., seeing is believing, and the way I see it, you can't show me much. Goodbye."

With that being said, Jasmine had fooled herself that she was the woman who was better off. Dr. T. had struck a nerve—a raw one that was painful. The nerve throbbed within the very core of Jasmine's being and was much too stinging to admit to at that moment. Jasmine sought the relationship coaching of a psychologist but was not ready for the truth.

"Jasmine, be that as it may, we're here to talk about you, not me. Now sit down and let's finish what we started. I know I confronted you in a manner that caught you off guard, but hear me out. You are a beautiful girl, and you deserve quality companionship. So be quiet and listen, so I can give you the answer you paid for. Oh, and by the way, I have been married for twenty years. I just don't wear my ring to work for instances like this."

Softened by the compliments and swayed by both the fact that she was indeed paying for answers and Dr. T's new found credibility, Jasmine obliged and sat down, this time listening as Dr. T. explained.

"The primary problem is not you, Jasmine. It is your dependency on your sex appeal to attract companionship. All the things you do to convey class men interpret as teasing. I don't dispute the fact that these men genuinely like you and I can see why, but the initial vibe of sex appeal frames how they view you—as a conquest, not a girlfriend. People are attracted to what you advertise. If you only advertise sex, why should you expect anything more?"

Although in psychological pain, Jasmine listened, but she rolled her eyes and began to withdraw. Sensing this, Dr. T. reached for her hands and asked, "Jasmine, answer this question. What else do you feel you have to offer a man besides being good eye candy and providing great sex?"

Jasmine crossed her legs, squirmed, fiddled with her purse straps, and anxiously twiddled her Nine West pump as she struggled to find an answer. She attempted to withdraw her hands in an effort to cross her arms but lost the will against Dr. T's caring grasp. Eventually, she lowered her guard, succumbed to the pressure to release her fears, and began to cry.

Jasmine indicated that she rarely spent much time thinking about it because it was too painful; however, after another fifteen minutes and a box of tissue, she eventually revealed that she doubted herself and feared that men would leave her altogether if she abandoned the one thing she knew she had; sex appeal.

Jasmine replied, "They will ignore me," but she stopped mid-sentence as she finally understood. "I do use sex as a crutch, and I blame men for taking it and leaving me hurt, lonely and used." "I guess the only real message I have been sending off all this time is that I'm sexy, desperate and unsure of myself."

This was the psychological breakthrough Jasmine needed to begin her healing. Over the next few months of counseling, Jasmine was able to regain her sense of self-worth and embark on a new way to go about seeking the love she so desperately desired.

Jasmine's story is familiar to many women who are pretty, smart and curvaceous, yet insecure and oblivious as to the real desires of men. Jasmine had good intentions, but her technique was flawed and misinformed.

Healthy dating is not about teasing, getting attention, or making men pursue you. It's about cultivating a friendship with a spirit of service and authenticity. Being real, supportive and using your inner beauty to impress opens the door to a lasting foundation- one that friendship, romance and marriage can now grow on.

A good friend captured it best with her words, "Love is friendship on fire." Friendship is the cornerstone of any good relationship. Whether it is romantic, family or business-related, friendship serves as the foundation to anchor the relationship.

One of the easiest ways to gain friendship is to be of service by supporting, listening to and exploring men's dreams and aspirations. While this sounds logical and simple, it is often overlooked and excluded from the process. Men may advertise a nice physique, money and sexual prowess but that is not all they want you to see. Get to know what is under the hood, and your man will be dedicated and thankful for life.

Likewise, a man may advertise that they are looking for a "dime-piece" or perfect ten, and great sex, but that's not what he really wants. Yes, he may even pressure or manipulate you to believe that he can "get it" anywhere. You figure, "Well, I might as well please him sexually to keep him at home because other women will certainly give in. I need to step my game up to keep him satisfied and from straying."

That sounds logical, but it is detrimental to your desire to be his exclusive girlfriend and eventual wife. What he really wants you to do is resist. Tell him, "Go *get it* then because I'm not compromising my standards." At this point, he will do one of two things; both are ultimately good for you. One, he will leave, which is good because he just revealed that you were in the "Let's Have Great Sex without Any Commitment Forever" box. Better to know up front than a full year later. Two, he will develop respect for you, increase his pursuit of you and catapult you to top priority because you were "the one" who didn't give in. In many ways, it is a test, and now you are sure to pass it every time!

For personal evidence, look back at your own failed relationships. Examine and explore one simple question: How much work and commitment did you mutually put into building a strong friendship before proceeding with sex? Now, I am certainly not saying that friendship and romance are mutually exclusive. In fact, a good friendship opens the door for romance; however, when you look at your more positive relationships, chances are that you invested a huge amount of time in your friendship and sex was secondary.

Dr. John Gottman is nationally considered the preeminent guru of marital research. He is author of *The Seven Principles for Making Marriage Work* and has conducted decades of research. Miraculously, he has designed studies that assess whether married couples will remain together or divorce. He credits the strength of the couple's friendship as being the single biggest factor to keeping couples together. Conversely, his research reveals that couples who decide to divorce inevitably list "lack of, or total loss of friendship" as the core of their problems.

Dr. Gottman's research makes a lot of sense when we reflect positively on our own friendships and positive relationships. Think about how much time, effort, sacrifice and energy went into building those relationships and the value they have for us as a result. We try our best to maintain these relationships despite conflict, hardship and life circumstances because they took so long to build. The positive memories, the hardships you were able to overcome together, the history of encouragement and the unconditional love and support have such value that you are super motivated to make things work despite significant conflict.

It would be devastating to lose a friendship with such rich memories, positive emotions and mutual connection. In addition, as we age, we realize that solid friendships are hard to replace. It takes years to build a friendship, so it is not as easy as just meeting someone new and moving on. Time, experience and mutual connection create a strong sense of chemistry that is difficult to replicate. Developing new friendships means that we must literally start over, and that is not something any of us look forward to doing.

The positive side is that once you take time to build solid friendships, the relationship is difficult to destroy. So why wouldn't you apply this principle to dating? You are looking for something enduring, solid and lifelong, right? Then focus your attention on being the best friend you can possibly be. Lovers are born out of friends, so focus on being a good, supportive friend, and you will have that diamond rock on your finger in no time.

When you shift your mindset toward friendship, good things will inevitably occur. One benefit is that it takes a lot of the pressure and disappointment out of dating. Dating to find friendship allows you to be more open-minded and less critical. You focus on appreciating your differences instead of being critical of one another.

The goal of any date is to connect and feel closer, getting to know your partner as the evening progresses. As you begin to share and support one another's world, you are working toward building a lasting foundation. Certainly, friendship is no guarantee for romance, but at least you are building the essential framework for it. At worst, you enjoy one another's company, learn something new or interesting, and have a new friend.

A quick word of caution: To build a successful, solid friendship, you must commit to being unyielding to lust and temptation. Lust is only temporary and will surely wane without solid friendship. Once the lust is gone, the relationship is over, and you have nothing to show for it but a good time. The lesson: You cannot build a marriage on sex and getting your needs met.

Now that you are convinced that friendship is a better foundation on which to build a relationship than sex, the logical next question needs to be explored. How exactly do you build this type of relationship, especially with the opposite sex? It is true; it is not as easy as it sounds.

Men can be difficult to engage in intimate conversation initially because they are keenly aware that women are trying to feel them out. They typically respond in one of two ways: 1) shut down or 2) tell you what they think you want to hear. It is as if they present you with a "representative," so they do not have to expose the real person until they get more information themselves.

Your time is valuable, and the selection of good men is slim, so you cannot afford to waste three months dating someone's representative, especially when you discover that you dislike the real person. You must learn how to distinguish Mr. Right from Mr. "I-Say-All-The-Right-Things." Waiting on a man to open up without prompting could take an eternity, which you do not have the luxury of if you desire to be married and have children anytime soon. Therefore, you must take control and assume the responsibility for getting a man to open up.

Find out what he is interested in, and ask genuine questions. Ask him about his ambitions in life, his ultimate career goals, and what his ideal girlfriend would look and act like. Try engaging him on a deeper level, and see how he responds. Don't hit him with rapid-fire questions that can simply be answered with a thoughtless yes or no. Instead, present situations and then listen to how he might handle them. If necessary, rephrase a question in a way that would be less threatening or that may appear as if you are an investigative reporter. Most men have colossal but fragile egos and will enjoy your keen interest in how they think and feel.

If you use engaging yet revealing questions, coupled with a warm spirit and friendly enthusiasm, men will begin to pour out their hearts. You'll be saying "TMI" (Too Much Information) instead of trying to pull teeth without anesthesia. In a day and age in which anything goes, you need as much information going into a relationship as you can possibly acquire. If you play your cards right, you'll only need one phone call or dinner conversation to gather enough data to decide if he is a keeper or to move on to the man behind door number two.

In case you need some assistance, included below is a set of questions specifically aimed at tapping into a deeper understanding and appreciation of your potential soul mate. Chances are that if you date long enough to answer most of these questions, you will be well on your way to building a lasting friendship and a budding romance. Try these questions for yourself.

Friendship Building Exercise

1) Where were you born and how does it affect your view of the world?

2) Who is your favorite musical artist and why?

3) Name three people you admire and tell me why.

4) What is your greatest success/failure?

5) What would you say is your source of strength?

6) To whom or where do you turn for guidance in your life?

7) What was your best/worst job?

8) What are the characteristics of an ideal friend?

9) Who was your best boy/girlfriend and why?

10) What is your greatest possibility/dream?

11) What is your greatest fear?

12) What hobbies do you like?

13) What stresses are you facing right now?

14) What do you do to relax and unwind?

15) Who is your favorite relative?

16) What is your favorite time of day for lovemaking?

17) What turns you on and off in a companion?

18) What is your favorite meal?

19) What personal improvements do you want to make in your life?

20) What is an ideal gift for you?

21) How would you prefer your companion to handle conflict?

22) What is your favorite way to spend an evening?

23) What are some of your concerns and worries?

24) What are some areas of your life of which you are presently unsure?

25) What is your favorite way to be soothed when you are upset?

26) Who was your best childhood friend and why?

27) What was your worst/best childhood experience?

28) What do you admire about your parents?

29) What things would you do differently from your parents?

30) What makes you an ideal companion for someone?

31) What was the last book you read, or what are you currently reading?

32) Do you have a major rival or enemy?

33) Who are your closest friends and why?

34) What personality traits would your parents and friends say you need to improve the most?

35) What motivates you to change?

36) Do you fear, love, or believe in God?

37) Do you have a secret ambition?

Again, you should not ask these questions in rapid-fire succession. Instead, you should gently weave them into the fabric of casual conversations. Be sure to listen intently to each answer. Affirm his responses; support his right to his opinions. Avoid becoming argumentative over responses you do not agree with. Lend eye contact. Watch his body language and facial expressions to determine if you have struck a nerve and should pull back for a while. Smile. Thank him for being honest with you.

You will find that checking under the hood will not only help you gain insight into the character and thoughts of your prospective mate, but will help you realize more about yourself as well. Using communication as the key, your understanding and sensitivity will unlock the door to really finding yourself some serious loving. Then, enjoy making up for lost time now that you have your own MR. RIGHT!

Formula SIX

DON'T HOPE TO GET MARRIED- EXPECT TO!
NEVER SETTLE FOR LESS THAN YOU DESERVE

"What's the point of dating someone who never wants to marry?" Dating places women in a precarious situation. Given the carnival-like dynamics of dating, you might end up on a dating carousel, dizzily whirling around without landing MR. RIGHT. Either you are not really into him, or he is not really into you.

Soon, the dating scene can feel like an endless cycle of unfulfilling rides that ultimately produce significantly less than what you want or deserve. It is no wonder that for thousands of women the dating scene can feel more like a raucous ride on a soul train instead of a wonderful journey to meet their soul mates.

If you are a woman who has consistently struggled with unfulfilling relationships, you may begin to question whether your MR. RIGHT even exists. This is heartbreaking because it ultimately signals a loss of hope and faith in God to create the perfect complement for you.

Dating is difficult because no matter how many men you meet, there is no guarantee that you will find what you desire most: love and marriage. All Internet dating and personal matchmaker services can offer is that you will meet someone, but they offer no guarantee for chemistry. While dating websites market your brilliance to a large network of people, none promises to produce your very own MR. RIGHT.

Sometimes you can date so much that you find yourself riding a soul train without even knowing it. For instance, some women have a tendency to seek out men who are the most sought after (i.e. music producers, club promoters, athletes, entertainers and other professionals).

There is certainly nothing wrong with aiming high; however, often times, these men sought out these careers because they provided glamour, money and accessibility to many women. Interestingly, many men within these industries eventually do settle down, but frequently it is with someone whom they had a previous relationship with before the fame and fortune.

Due to the perception that MR. RIGHTS are in limited supply, many women are feeling the pressure to go into battle to compete for a soul mate. With this mindset, stress, conflict and self-doubt are bound to flourish, thereby creating the ultimate lose-lose situation. You can work hard competing with other women to eventually win the top spot but still not win his heart. Eventually, you realize that you spent precious time, energy, and love battling for a man who had no desire to settle down, although you hoped that he would eventually settle down once you won the prized top spot.

It can be heartbreaking and disillusioning to realize that the top spot does not include marriage. His mindset is that he worked hard to achieve his professional status and deserves a lifestyle of partying, flirting and being with beautiful women. If you are not careful, you could easily find yourself steaming mad when you realize that you spent your prime years in pursuit of a man who never intended to become the husband you were prepping him to be or deserve.

Age also creates dating stress when you have failed to find MR. RIGHT as planned. It is quite natural to feel nervous and even desperate when the ideal age to marry and bear children comes and goes. Making matters worse, family and friends are constantly questioning your relationship status and trying to hook you up with any man with a pulse.

Thus, it is quite understandable that the idea of finding MR. RIGHT becomes a foreign idea and is eventually replaced with the notion of settling for "MR. JUST-GOOD-ENOUGH." The more time that passes, the more tempting it becomes to lower your standards and settle for company over long-term loneliness. After all, you fear that MR. RIGHT may never really exist.

I have spoken with a number of eligible women who express this sense of regret. "Maybe I've concentrated so much on finding that 'perfect package' that I let some pretty good guys go. I'm praying that I didn't make a mistake," captures their sentiments.

To be honest, after listening to so many of them, I conceded that they had a valid point. At what age or point in life do you begin to reassess what you want and make adjustments? When you are not in a meaningful relationship at thirty, thirty-five or forty, do you begin to take what you can get out of fear of a lifetime of loneliness? This is a very real and pressing question for thousands of women. Frankly, I began to wonder if I was wrong to continue to encourage women to hold out until they found their MR. RIGHT; however, after meeting Erika and hearing her story, I am more convinced than ever that the answer is an emphatic NO!

Erika was a robust sister in her late thirties who hailed from Pittsburg, Pennsylvania. She was a thick sister who weighed approximately 170 pounds and was 5'7" tall. Erika was an impressive woman who knew how to dress to enhance her full figure. The country boys would lust over her because she had some meat on her bones. She was not shy about accenting her wonderful thighs and busty chest, yet everything Erika did was with class.

Because of Erika's personality and flair, she rarely had problems meeting men. In fact, she had frequent contact with men who were handsome, professional and considerate. Despite being in their late thirties, these men had absolutely no desire to settle down and preferred the bachelor lifestyle; however, these men were "atypical" bachelors. They were not preoccupied with sex and could date long-term with or without being intimate.

One particular guy, Marshall, treated Erika like a queen. Marshall was a computer programmer from Knoxville, Tennessee. He wore collared shirts that still managed to reveal his muscular physique. His silver-trimmed glasses gave him the look of a professor you wouldn't mind staying after class with. He had no children, had never been married, was a great cook and was an all-around nice guy.

Erika and Marshall had the luxury of excellent chemistry, enjoyed one another's company, and made no secret of their genuine and sincere care for one another. They were the best of friends and enjoyed a variety of social outings together. They attended one another's company holiday parties, spent Valentine's Day together, and even took summer vacations together. They dated for almost a year with no commitment. Initially Erika figured that time would bring Marshall closer to the light, but after the second Christmas party with no commitment, it didn't appear that she was any closer to marriage than the first day they met.

Before now, Erika had been quiet, opting to allow time to reveal Marshall's intentions; however, after her thirty-eighth birthday, she decided it was time for some answers. Her biological clock was ticking and Marshall appeared to be plum deaf. Shortly after eating her birthday cake with nothing special to celebrate, she expressed her concerns to Marshall. She wondered whether she was lacking something or was doing something wrong. He denied any major issues with her and said that he was content with the pace and status of their current relationship.

Reflecting on past relationships, Erika wondered what she was doing to attract men who all appeared to belong to the same club: The AAU club—Awesome, Available yet Uninterested in marriage. Marshall indicated that he enjoyed the intimacy of their current relationship, thought she would be a great wife and failed to offer any negatives; however, he was emphatic that he did not want to marry and become "tied down" by one woman. This didn't make any sense to Erika because Marshall even admitted that he hadn't dated anyone else for over a year. The more Marshall spoke, the more confused, frustrated, and angry Erika became.

"What is this all about?" she lamented to her girlfriends and mom, who were equally confused. "I could understand if he wanted to date other women, didn't love me, or didn't believe in monogamy, but he's saying everything is fine. I just don't get it."

Sadly, Marshall represents a growing bastion of men who simply want to have their cake and eat it too. The real but unacceptable truth is that Marshall wanted the freedom to do as he pleased despite rarely, if ever, exercising this option. He was perfectly comfortable with the idea of dating Erika without an official title for the rest of his life and was under no pressure to change. Marshall's words hit Erika like a ton of bricks. She knew he might not be ready for marriage now, but to hear him utter the word *never* was indigestible.

She desperately wanted to be married and had not given up on the miracle of children; however, she considered her age and the amount of time she had invested in Marshall and made a critical decision. She decided that a "just good-enough" companion was better than loneliness and agreed to accept Marshall's way of doing things. For a while, she was happy.

They met each other's family, went on vacations, and even moved in together; however, Erika was soon unhappier than ever. She couldn't help but feel that something was missing, something huge. As it turned out, the more time she spent with Marshall, the more she wanted the whole enchilada!

After a year and a half of no progress, Erika made the long-overdue decision to call it quits with Marshall. This was an incredibly hard decision because she almost had it all: a good man, loving companionship and a good friend. The only thing missing was marriage. She decided that matrimonial commitment was too important to compromise. Since her life-long desire was for marital bliss and union, she could no longer commit to someone who was emphatic about not sharing her dream. If she remained committed to Marshall, she would be unavailable to meet MR. RIGHT who was interested in getting married.

It took Erika months to get used to the idea and reality of being single again. Ironically, she was happier because she no longer had to accept the unfulfilling reality of a lifetime of settling for less than she deserved. What she shared with me about the source of her happiness resonated, and I pray that it does the same for you. She shared that, for the first time in her life, she began to look at dating in a new light. If she met someone intriguing, she would dive in enthusiastically. If she didn't, she could just as easily enjoy her own company or the company of good friends.

The change in Erika's life was amazing. When she stopped looking for dates, she actually got more of them—and great ones too! She realized that during previous years, she was making dating harder than it needed to be. When she learned to be patient and wait on God to produce the man she deserved, she was able to relax and truly cherish herself.

Strange as it may seem, Erika was actually happier than ever before. She still went to the movies, on vacations with friends and family and on occasional dates. Most importantly, she learned to enjoy her own company. She realized that over the last seven years she had been putting so much emphasis on finding a soul mate that she had forgotten to "date" herself. She wrestled with physical intimacy needs but was ultimately happier in the end.

Over time, Erika made a very important discovery in her life; she could be happy with or without a man. She felt like an eight-point-five on a scale of ten in terms of relationship happiness. She acknowledged the reality that she would likely jump to a ten once she found that special MR. RIGHT who was willing to commit to marriage; however, she was now more convinced than ever that being an eight-point-five alone was better than feeling like a five with MR. JUST GOOD ENOUGH. If the relationship had no potential for eventual marital bliss, she was simply not interested in participating.

Erika represents thousands of women in this world who have yet to meet their MR. RIGHT; however, she also epitomizes the spirit of patience and faith necessary to deserve her coming blessing. At present, Erika is gleefully and patiently waiting on her soul mate and is excited about having the opportunity for a deeply satisfying marriage. Regardless of how much time passes, she refuses to settle for "just good enough" ever again.

She is happy and content with her life now, but you know who has started calling again... Marshall. Over time, Erika realized that it was never about Marshall in the first place. She had played by his rules without asserting hers. Marshall could call all he wanted, but this was a new day because, now, it was all about what *she* wanted. Marshall expressed that he missed her and was now interested in discussing Erika's desire for commitment. As it turns out, one of the fruits of her self-exploration was the realization of just how REMARKABLE a woman she truly was. She wasn't the only one who noticed either—so did Marshall.

In summary, men don't like to lose three things: love, power and respect. When Erika left Marshall, he ended up losing all three, which was more than he could bear. Ultimately, he lost her love, her daily attention *and* the power to have his cake and eat it too. Ironically, he is now fighting to reacquire that love, attention and respect. I'll have to admit that Erika's chances for love look pretty good now. In fact, she has another suitor who is madly in love with her, and she is enjoying every moment of it. Look who is having her cake and eating it too now!

If there is one thing I want you to get from this book, it is that you don't have to settle for "good enough."

You deserve to find and enjoy a lifetime of happiness with your soul mate. As you embark on your journey toward love, do so with passion, the highest of expectations, supreme self-confidence and patience that everything will work out according to God's plan. It is OK to ask God for encouragers and signs that you are on the right track because He rejoices in those who demonstrate faith and patience. Try to avoid allowing negativity and impatience to ruin your blessing. Accept the fact that true faith requires that you remain radiant, joyful and hopeful even when MR. RIGHT is nowhere in sight.

The ability to remain joyfully patient and radiant is revealed in obtaining a divine understanding of faith. Faith is defined as the "spiritual substance" inside you that can either grow or wane. The Bible defines faith as the substance of things hoped for and the evidence of things not seen (*Hebrews 11:1*).

God is saying that the source of power, happiness and overall prosperity is in believing in Him; it is not of human control or design. *Hebrews 11:1* teaches that you cannot navigate this quest by sight! I know you would certainly love to pick your soul mate according to your own timetable but this would be like trying to control nature. You have no control over when the sun rises or sets, and you certainly have no power over when you will attract MR. RIGHT. You must trust that you will but on God's timing.

God will take care of your need for relationship and connection. This requires faith, which is "blind" because you cannot see it or predict the outcome. Your continued belief and positive attitude are pleasing to God and your faith will be rewarded in abundance, similar to Erika. There are thousands of phenomenal women who avoided the temptation to settle for less than they deserved and were rewarded with finding and marrying MR. RIGHT. They now enjoy a supremely joyous married life, complete with children and self-assurance that they made the right decision. You can applaud them and smile yourself because you are next!

Application Section

One of the greatest travesties is not realizing your worth. Just because men fail to articulate your worth doesn't mean that they don't recognize it. Sometimes, it is necessary for you to do a self-evaluation to remind yourself just how dynamic, unique and special you are. When it comes to getting and staying married, confidence is the key.

"Men can find eye candy all day while confident women are in limited supply"

Thus, it's time to put in work on maintaining our confidence so that you can resist the temptation of ever settling for anything less than a man who wishes to spend his entire life with you. Before you can begin to make sure that your man is the perfect fit, you must take time to actually envision the kind of man that you want to complement. Just like everything else in life, planning gets you to your destination faster than lack thereof. Your strategy to finding Mr. RIGHT cannot be to date as many men as necessary to find the right fit. Men are not shoes!

"You cannot date men like you try on shoes."

You cannot obtain what you cannot first see. In other words, if you don't know what Mr. Right looks like then how are you going to recognize him when he introduces himself to you? It's like shoes: you must first know your size to determine the right fit. If you resort to trying on men without knowing your type, you'll endure a lifetime of discomfort, pain and rejection. Trying on a man who doesn't fit your ideal for Mr. Right is like thinking that your feet won't swell after you run a marathon in some six inch heels. Men, like shoes, that don't fit… HURT!

Besides, I'll whisper this so that no one can hear," *Men don't like women who have tried on a lot of shoes."* You will save yourself a lot of time, energy and self-respect if you invest in thinking about what kind of man best complements you before you leave the house to find him. This strategy will keep you out of places that don't match your brand and out of shoes that could harm your soul indefinitely. After all, you are a more efficient shopper if you know exactly what you are looking for and where to find it before you start. So, let's begin.

In four pages, please describe the qualities, appearance, and essence of the man you wish to soon marry. If already married, describe the man you wish for your husband to transform into.

loves to look at me and
flirt w/me. loves to cook and
stay home. Works for himself
for flexibility. loves his family
and knows how to properly
distance people. Is open

and honest. lets me know how he feels w/out stepping out of the relationship. Serious about his business. likes fine classy things such as a good cigar and glass of whiskey. likes to play golf and loves to spend time w/ me. wants children with me and only me. teaches me. taller than I am. thick build but no fat. Healthy and cares about his health. Humble and God fearing and loving. Don't talk too much - mild mannered.

Congratulations, you have now saved yourself some valuable time because you now know exactly who you are looking for. If you are with that man then it's now time to make sure that you value one another equally to keep the love flourishing and moving toward or maintaining that ring status. Let's make sure that you are not doing too much or giving to little to ensure that you continue to fit one another as your relationship grows.

Write out a list of your virtues and the many ways that you improve and support your man.

1) I can cook

2) I'm not lazy - help meat

3) I Keep my body and health intact.

4) I support my man w/ sharing cooking ideas.

5) I support him in if he has things to do. I don't complaine.

6) I uplift him

7) ______

8) ______

Now write out a list of your partner's virtues and ways that he improves and supports you.

1) he can cook

2) he is disciplined

3) he helps me invest

4) he teaches me about me

5) he does not like to yell

6) ______________________

7) ______________________

8) ______________________

Is your list equal? Share your list with your man and illicit his feedback to make sure you agree about the list. Next, make the list equal by either doing less or asking him to do more. Do not continue the relationship until your lists are almost identical. You may need to do this monthly to keep things balanced.

Men respond better to logic versus emotion. When you

show them how much they are slacking in the relationship, they are much more likely improve than if you simply stop communicating with them, withhold loving or argue with him. If your man responds, then let the good times roll. If he does not, then he has proven to be a selfish lover and it may be time to seek counseling or leave and find a better one.

Never settle for less than you deserve in relationships. You won't respect yourself and neither will he.

Formula SEVEN

MAKE MY MOMMA (and EX's) LIKE YOU
MAKE HIS LIFE EASIER NOT HARDER

"Learning to master a man's family makes you part of it." It was Friday night. Keisha and Darren were enjoying a romantic, candlelight dinner at home. The Sauvignon Blanc was flowing, and Keisha and Darren were enjoying one another's company and the delectable lobster tail they had prepared together.

Keisha was a beauty from Tallahassee, Florida. Her eyes had an Asian appeal and were coupled with a radiant smile, deep dimples and long, curly hair that cascaded down the middle of her back.

Darren was from Philadelphia. He had that typical Northern bravado and was a bit of a pretty boy. At times, he could be very assertive and dominant, but he was genuinely a nice guy.

At the beginning of their relationship, Darren exhibited a temperamental disposition, and Keisha never knew which Darren she was going to experience: the gentle, soft, and loving middle-school principal or the dominant, assertive and forceful former basketball star from Philly by way of the Chicago streets.

Both Keisha and Darren had experienced successive high-stress weeks at work and were starving to unwind in the peace and quiet of one another's arms. After a few rounds of footsy under the table, Darren decided that, for dessert, he would quench his insatiable desire with a little of Keisha's sweetness. Keisha was being seductive as she prepared to serve him up a piece of her own hot apple pie when someone rang the doorbell. Peeping through the window, they recognized a frequent visitor—Darren's mom. Annoyed by the uninvited guest, Keisha's demeanor soured. Every ounce of passion she felt immediately turned to white, hot anger.

"Oh, how nice it would be if I could just enjoy my man without having to deal with his crazy mother," she mused silently. Darren's mood changed as well as he anticipated the drama that would ensue.

"Darren, why can't you tell your mother to call before she decides to just pop over?"

A bit embarrassed and on the defensive, Darren responded in his usual manner. "Baby, you know how my mother is. Hurry and clean up those dishes." His assertive personality pushed its way to the forefront, and there was no room for argument.

Feeling helpless and close to tears, Keisha decided enough was enough. Not only did she *not* clean up the dishes, she was determined to confront Darren's mother for the last time.

"Mrs. Mitchell, so good to see you…again," Keisha injected in the highest, most sarcastic voice she could muster as Darren's mother entered the house.

"Oh, *you're* here again. You need to be paying rent," Darren's mom mumbled under her breath. It was as if a stick of dynamite was tossed into the room. As if someone had rung the bell on the *Jerry Springer* show, Keisha and Mrs. Mitchell were trading ugly barbs and Darren was caught in the middle, unable to control the fray between the two women he loved. They went round for round until, just like on *Jerry Springer*, the moment came when Darren had to choose between Keisha and his dear sweet mama. As was to be expected, Keisha ended up losing the battle, leaving with an air of rudeness that included a stinging insult for the both of them and a wall-rattling slam of the door.

Darren and Keisha's arguments over his mother had escalated to an unhealthy pitch. They had only minor issues and differing philosophies about child rearing and finances, but Darren's mother was the potential relationship breaker. Keisha was adamant that Darren had to choose either his mom or her. She felt that if Darren were serious about marriage that his loyalty should lie with his future wife.

"Darren, every time your mom comes around, you revert back to being a wimpy little boy who runs behind his mother's skirt. I expect you to step up and be a man who is willing to side with the woman you claim you want to be your future wife."

"Baby, you know I can't do that," Darren would counter, being ever mindful of the bond between his mom and her only son.

All right, ladies, take your sides! In case you want to know the answer, Keisha is going to lose! In principle, she is correct, but her methods are bound for failure. There is no man in his right mind who is going to choose any woman over his mother -- the same woman who nursed, fed and built him up. He can't be expected consciously to choose someone *over* her. Keisha was in the deep end of the pool without a life jacket and was being sucked into the drain. I am sure the lobster tail and loving were great, but they were certainly no match against the loyalty to dear old mom.

There is no room for competition when girlfriends and moms are involved. One of the biggest myths out there is that a man needs to choose between his mom and his girlfriend/wife. That makes for a guaranteed lose-lose situation. Hence, the only harmonious choice is to join forces.

Keisha does have a point, though. Darren is no longer a little boy, and his mom should respect his privacy and their relationship; however, Darren's mom obviously reigns supreme, so if Keisha wants an enduring relationship with Darren, she is going to have to get permission from the first lady first.

Mothers are protective of their children, especially their sons, and they have very specific ideas about the type of woman they want their sons to marry. If the road to a man's heart is through his stomach, the way to a smooth relationship, without family interference, is through acceptance by his mother.

Let's examine the mother's perspective. It is most beneficial for her to have a good relationship with her son's wife, just as she would want her husband to respect her father. Most mothers, especially ones without daughters, dream of having a mother-daughter bond with their son's wife. Remember, marriage is not just between two people -- it is a connection between two distinct families. The mom is the queen of the family, and if she objects to the relationship, it is going to be like pushing a boulder uphill. Somebody is going to get a hernia.

So what is a woman to do? Fake acceptance of mom's intrusions, or allow her to continue to disrespect the boundaries? Neither. Instead, learn to become the family psychologist! A woman who is able to be the peacemaker, diplomatically dealing with his mother, will win the undying love and appreciation from her man. A man is acutely aware of the quirks in his mother's personality. His greatest wish is for his woman to befriend her. Nothing sounds like music to a man's ears more than hearing his mother say, "I just love (insert your name). She's adorable; she's a keeper." When you win the stamp of approval from his mom, you are in, and more than lobster and good loving only time separates you from marriage.

Here are some tips to befriending Mom. As you already know, the key to any relationship is spending quality time together. Adjust your mindset so that you will do everything in your power to make her like you, not by being fake but by focusing on her needs. Moms will test you because they want to see how you respond under stress. They are aware of the antics of women, and how you respond can make or break you.

Let's roll back the video on Keisha and Darren and redo that dinner scene. Keisha and Darren are just about to have dessert when someone rings the doorbell. Darren looks out the window and sees that it is his mother. This time, Keisha smiles. "Wow, there's Mom again. Offer her some dessert while I clear the dishes before she has a meltdown."

They both chuckle, knowing Mom's obsession with cleanliness. Darren smiles and gratefully says, "Thanks Babe, I'll try to get rid of her as soon as I can."

"That's OK, Darren; we can always continue where we left off after she leaves. After all, we will have a lifetime together."

Ladies, can I tell you that any woman who responds like that is in for the best loving of her life? You are fine, sexy, smart, an excellent cook and you accept his overbearing mother? Now that's a package too good to pass up. When his mother comes in, be cordial and love her the way he does.

"Mrs. Mitchell, good to see you again. You are just in time. We were just finishing dinner." Moms are impressed with a woman who can cook and nurture their boy. "Join us for some dessert. I have homemade apple pie in the oven. I know it's not as good as yours, but..."

Mom hesitates as Keisha springs into action with pie and saucer in hand. She says coyly, "Darren would you like a piece?" smiling at her clever play on words.

"Of course I'll have a HOT piece," Darren replies as they share a private laugh.

Before long, Mrs. Mitchell is complimenting Keisha on her pie and offering tips on how to make a flakier crust. This is not the time for Keisha to get offended. This is a test and one she had better pass. Mom is testing to see if Keisha is going to allow her to have any influence in their relationship. If Keisha gets defensive, she is as good as gone; however, if she responds with loving acceptance, she will be in for life.

"I'm sorry Mrs. Mitchell; I warned you it wasn't as good as yours. What's it missing?" Mom will inevitably offer her favorite recipe. Keisha takes her plate, giving the appearance that a clean house is important.

If you follow this method, you will make his mom an ally. She will be your biggest supporter, even when her son begins to act up. If she likes you, she will call and straighten him out if he is taking too long to produce that ring; however, you must be sincere. The next time you are making an apple pie, or any special meal, make sure you call her for input. Chances are that you will enjoy your conversations and begin to build a bridge that connects to her son's heart. Once you get Mom on your side, the only thing left for you to do is throw the rice.

Now that we have dealt with dear old Mom, it's time to concentrate on the ex-wives, ex-girlfriends and babies' mamas. If you don't have to deal with these elements consider yourself lucky; however, in today's society where divorce, out-of-wedlock children, and women opting to be "sideline" women are prevalent, it is likely that you will have to experience some form of interaction. The philosophy behind dealing with all of these women is the same, so we can put them into one group: Not his wife.

Since none of these women currently holds the position you have already claimed, it is time for you to act like it. If you really expect to marry this man, you must change your mindset. These women are no longer competition. Understand that there can be no competition if the prize already has been won. If you view these other women as competition, you inadvertently put yourself on their level, which is what they need to claim the prize. Don't do that under any circumstance. Your actions will inevitably open up the competition when you could have claimed the prize and sent the unlucky contestants home without a parting gift.

Ex-wives and babies' mothers can be difficult to deal with and can strain a relationship if you allow it to happen. The best way to deal with them is to exhibit supreme confidence, class and love. Their relationship with your man is over, so treat it as such. Their relationship is one based solely on co-parenting. In today's age of blended families, there are many occasions that require two families to come together for the good of the child (birthdays, holidays, school performances, doctor's appointments, etc.). However, you have to be secure in your role to make it work successfully. Regardless of what feelings or behavior the other co-parent may have, remain secure in your royal position within the family.

An important step to ensuring peace and harmony is to take control of the situation. Recommend to your man that his child, the child's mother and the rest of the family come over for a holiday meal. Now, of course, they will not spend the night and most will not want to; however, the fact that you are confident enough to host the holiday dinner with the blended family clearly establishes your superior role to all. Because this is new, relatives will initially be skeptical and come with both eyes open to any funny business; however, as you confidently serve and play the wifely role of super hostess, all the pieces will fall into place.

The ex-wife will clearly observe your position in your man's life. She will be forced to realize that you don't feel threatened by her presence, and she'll appreciate that you care for her child's happiness. Of course, be aware of your role when the child's mother is around, and always defer to her judgment regarding her child. Ask permission to give the child a present, pick them up or play with them. Mothers are very protective and despite preferring that you did not exist, would rather have a cordial versus hostile relationship with you. By being assertive and creating an air of respect, you have a good chance of taking her off the defensive. You can begin to form at least a cordial relationship, which will send a wonderful message to your stepchild that blended families don't have to fight.

How should you handle those vindictive ex-girlfriends, babies' mamas, and ex-wives? Be aware that the road will be a little rockier but you must handle it in a similar manner. Some women are still bitter and may be evil enough to show up at the holiday dinner with the intention of ruining things; however, she no longer has the power unless you give it to her. If she becomes overly controlling of her child (like telling the child that she can't play with you), just show that you are the bigger person by remaining calm and respecting her right to act a fool.

As your mother probably told you, "One monkey doesn't stop the show." The ex will soon realize that what she is doing is trifling and will eventually calm down. Additionally, the child, father and entire family will work on your behalf to minimize the mom's negativity. When this happens, she will realize that she has no chance of disrupting the wonderful bond you have with your man and the family. She will have to make a choice to either calm down and play by your rules or simply drop her child off without drama. Either way you win; however, you must always maintain your cool because she's looking for some evidence of weakness, and getting you upset is exactly what she's hoping to do. By staying cool, you render her powerless, and she will have to respect you for "not going there" and allowing her to act a fool without participating.

Congratulations! You now have the power to handle any family issue that may arise. The key to "eliminating" the competition for your man is not to create any. Your man will follow your lead and dismiss whoever cannot respect and play by your rules. If you are lucky, you won't have to do a thing if you remain calm and play your cards right.

Furthermore, always allow God to guide your actions. By doing so, no weapon, ex-girlfriend, mother or baby's mama for that matter, formed against you will prosper. Your man will be most appreciative and be forced to see you as "one of a kind," which means you are irreplaceable. You want to make sure your man feels, "Where in the world am I going to find another woman who can deal with my mama, ex-wife and/or baby's mama so effectively?" He will love you even more for being a secure woman.

Not only are you his lover, friend and nurturer, but you are also his and the family's psychologist. This makes you a quadruple threat! You become the cherry on top of the pie a la mode with whipped cream. Now that is hard to replace, so rejoice and walk with confidence because he is not going anywhere except outside to wash your car.

Even if that man is dumb enough to leave, he'll be running back in no time once he compares you to whatever downgrade he made. The funny thing is, even his family will tell him that he's stupid! You have this situation under control—lock, stock, and barrel. You go girl!

THREE-PART BONUS CHAPTER:

A WOMAN'S QUEST FOR LOVE

PART ONE: "ALONE & BETRAYED"

"Every woman experiences a period where she questions if and when her next relationship will appear." Flirting is an art and should be incorporated into every woman's ring formula. Flirting is defined as playfully or purposefully trying to attract the admiration and attention of men for self-gratification. Many definitions of the word have a negative connotation but I couldn't disagree more. Flirting, when done properly, can give any woman the power she needs to control the dating scene by selecting the man she wants to pursue her.

Are you tired of men you have no interest in continuously ruining your mood, wasting your time and blocking your ability to attract man you desire with their tired, unsolicited game? How would you like to be able to take control and only attract quality men? How would you like to substitute the process of waiting, hoping and praying that the fine man you are interested in notices you with a formula that allows you to purposely draw his attention, affection and admiration in your direction? If you answered yes, yes and yes then you better learn how to F.L.I.R.T.

F.L.I.R.T is an acronym for Fun, Loving, Interesting & Intriguing, Revealing, and Touching the man you wish to court you. When you are able to master this technique with the skilled of a master painter then you will enjoy power and attention like never before. You can finally relax because you will have acquired a skill that gives you the upper hand when it comes to attracting men and evoking them to meet, court, commit and marry you. The only thing you will have to wait on is the right man.

Women hold a psychological advantage over men because you possess what men desire. Men are hard-wired to constantly strive for more. They work hard for more money, more power, more excitement, more control and more love.

What's interesting is that men will work harder, longer, smarter, stronger and wiser just for the *chance* to have more. In fact, the chase is so exhilarating that men report enjoying the chase more than actually attaining the object of their affection sometimes. Hence, men need to chase to be happy. Men can neither chase themselves nor any object that is still. Thus, by the process of deduction ladies, men need you to make them chase you!

From the previous chapters, you have already learned to take inventory and make yourself a unique asset. Now, it's time for you to put those assets to work to attract the man you desire into your life. While some men are fools with their money and their women by carelessly neglecting their assets, good men, by contrast, cherish, nurture and guard over their assets until death does them part. For a variety of reasons, some men do not see women as assets, only liabilities. Hence, they choose to purposely mislead, manipulate and use women for their own self-gratification.

Women who make the mistake of pursuing men who do not value assets always get played. Unfortunately, there are some women who think that a man's status, money, and/or possessions (gold) make him an asset. The goal is to befriend him and sexually please to gain access to his gold so that she, in turn, can feel golden. The problem with this strategy is that it makes the man the source for happiness and not the woman. Unfortunately, gold-diggers only strategy is to dig for men's gold. However, a Ring Formula woman knows that she *is* gold and never needs to dig a day in her life- that's why her nails stay clean. In fact, all she needs to do is shine and allow men to find her, time and time again.

I understand why some women choose gold-digging as a temporary strategy for finding happiness and love. The answer is simple. They are not yet convinced that *they* are the prize and, thus, must resort to extraordinary, external measures to find a sense of self-worth. Despite possessing what the world deems as superficial beauty, they lack the inner beauty and self-confidence necessary to keep great men happy.

Women who choose to dig for gold usually attract male suitors but only for a season or two. They fail to realize is that men are hard-wired to pursue assets and their take-take-take mentality makes them the ultimate liabilities. Some men are initially wooed by their superficial beauty but will always distance themselves from these types of women over time because they decrease the overall value of the man. Because of their negative qualities they are like kryptonite and force men to drop them from the portfolio to avoid losing further power and assets.

I empathize with women who have experimented with the gold-digging approach to finding love, companionship and self-value because statistics show that an absent, neglectful and/or abusive dad, ex-boyfriend or sibling is the primary culprit for stealing their self-worth in the first place.

Additionally, as a Christian, I do not wish to judge since that is reserved for the Creator. You are still my sisters and, hopefully, will benefit from some positive insight from a man who sincerely loves women. By using this chapter, I wish to empower you to use a more effective strategy, F.L.I.R.T.

Before you dismiss this chapter as one only for women with a low sense of self-worth, read on because this chapter applies to any woman who has ever been dumped, questioned her own self-worth, questioned why men don't choose her, or wondered if she was special enough to be married. Additionally, this chapter is for any woman who simply wishes to take control over attracting good men into her life and increase her chances of marriage.

Let's face it, being lonely and helplessly waiting for attention from a quality man can be extremely frustrating. This frustration is intensified when your core group of girlfriends enter into relationships and are all out dating on the weekends. You feel weird about going out alone which leaves you at home on the weekends waiting on the right man to find you, if he finds you.

That strategy yields little power over finding a mate and frustrates potentially marriage-minded suitors because they are ready to marry but cannot find that special someone to make them stop looking. If you don't remember anything else you read, remember this, "A good man will not pass up an opportunity to meet a great asset because he needs that woman to ultimately be his wife."

Men seek to marry and then find the woman who is convinced that she is the unique asset worthy of being his wife. When he meets her, he feels lucky no matter how much money, fame or fortune he enjoyed before because she is the ultimate asset and the prize he desires above all else. Thus, he changes his behavior and readies himself to pursue, obtain and gain the love of the woman he intends to marry.

He is determined to stop at no end until she accepts his ring and hand in marriage. In fact, some men will go through extraordinary lengths to find the one because, in the end, it's worth it if she becomes his wife. Don't believe me? Ask Summer how she met Doc.

Summer was the kind of woman that all men wished for. She possessed characteristics that were oxymoronic but magically seemed to work for her. She was sexy yet very conservative. She loved to party but only with her man. She had a great set of girlfriends but was primarily interested in hooking them up with her man's friends (only the good ones). She loved to listen to rap music but attended church religiously and never cursed.

She was adventurous but refused to ever disrespect herself. She was bold enough to have a pet snake and tarantula but loved children. She could watch a boxing match with the guys on Friday night and still hang out at the Farmer's Market with her grandmother on Saturday morning.

Summer was a prototype; the kind of woman that men thought no longer existed. She was a perfect mixture of old and new school. She had a dress fetish and loved to give clothes the opportunity to share her body. Yet, she picked the place where she purchased them based on their support of ovarian cancer (Tootsies.com).

She aspired to be prosperous by working hard and empowering others. She saved her money wisely and preferred to prepare home-cooked meals over dining out. In fact, she would actually get upset if anyone else (outside of his mother) fed her man. She expected to be wined and dined but only relative to her man's budget. She valued creativity over flash.

Summer had everything a man was looking for but like so many quality women in this world, she did not have a man. She used to have a man but that relationship ended when he stopped valuing her. Although the decision to reenter the single scene was tough, the idea of settling for less love than she gave was even scarier. Summer had the beautiful benefit of having a very strong relationship with her father. The oldest of three girls, Summer was the first to benefit from her dad's perfect blend of affection and strict rules about dating.

Her father had only one rule: "Conduct yourself like my daughter at all times and only date men who reflect my character". Thus, men who did not submit to God, demonstrate chivalry, value education or believe in being providers need not apply. Her father was notorious for giving potential suitors the riot act to see how they responded under pressure to ensure that his daughters were in capable, caring and respectful hands.

Summer never complained because she trusted her father and reaped the benefits of being treated with respect. After all, no man in his right mind wanted to disappoint "father" after receiving the riot act. Guys who were eager to bed her before wouldn't even go in for a kiss without father's blessing.

The most interesting quality about Summer was that she seemed to be immune to feeling lonely. Don't get me wrong, she preferred to be in a committed relationship but could easily enjoy time with her family, friends and dating. In fact, she enjoyed dating so much that she developed a reputation as a "serial dater". Due to her beautiful spirit, she was convinced that men should want to spend time with her. She was cleverly aware of men's ulterior motives but handled them with the skill of a psychologist. Summer was not a doctor but she might as well have been because she knew everything about flirting to attract a quality suitor.

Summer was an avid reader and voraciously consumed books in the self-help genre. She was especially fond of books about relationships and finding love. While confident in her own abilities, she was not the type to miss an opportunity to learn something new. Summer was competitive by nature and naturally wanted to be the best girlfriend and eventual wife that she could possibly be. She had the benefit of watching her mother take amazing care of her father and saw first-hand just how much value a woman has in a man's life. She also saw the benefits of being a devoted wife by observing the variety of ways her father took care of her mother in return.

Summer wanted what her parents had and was convinced that she would find it. She had a strong faith in God and trusted him to send the right man at the right time. However, she was getting a little anxious though because it was going on a full two years of being outside of a committed relationship. Additionally, all but one of her girlfriends was in committed relationships that appeared on the fast track to marriage.

The only single girlfriend she had left to hang out with on the weekends was her best friend Meagan. They would have fun visiting different jewelry shops on the weekends picking out future wedding rings for one another. They had it all figured it out. Whichever one of them was not getting married would help the husband to be to pick out their pre-selected ring and while the other would act surprised. The two would often joke about which one of them would get married first and who would be the last old maid of the crew.

Meagan was an extremely attractive woman with a slender build who possessed a smile that would light up a room but it didn't indicate her actual mood. Meagan was a true chameleon who could easily mask her true feelings in a moment's notice- a defense mechanism she learned as a child. Meagan didn't like where her life was headed. She had initially experienced a string of promising relationships after college but found herself now five years removed from one.

In fact, she had been taken advantage of numerous times after losing her last true love, David, to an untimely relocation to Afghanistan due to the war. She loved David plenty but not enough to abandon her career, friends and family to live in a foreign country thousands of miles away. The two would often talk about that decision with Summer confirming that she made the right decision despite missing David dearly. However, neither could deny that Meagan began to change the day David left.

It had been almost five years but Summer was growing more concerned for her friend because she seemed to be growing weaker versus coping better. Meagan was becoming increasingly more superficial, buying designer clothes and shoes instead of actively paying down her college loans. She also noticed that Meagan was becoming more distant and began hanging with another set of girlfriends. Being the ultimate girlfriend, Summer tried to join Meagan with her new crew but she simply didn't fit. As much as Summer didn't want to say it, Meagan was associating and becoming a gold-digger.

Summer and Meagan had been best friends for ten years and both opted not to discuss their differences to avoid conflict. However, there relationship was becoming more strained as the months went by. Summer developed a predictable pattern of finding excuses not to hang out with Meagan and her friends on the weekends. Instead of telling Meagan to change her friends, Summer decided to take a passive approach and spend more time at home reading for enjoyment while Meagan and her new crew hit the streets.

What Summer didn't know was that Meagan was becoming increasingly angrier because she felt her best friend was purposely judging and rejecting her instead of remaining loyal to her BFF (Best Friend Forever) of ten years. With dogged determination, Meagan decided she had enough and invited Summer to have breakfast at her favorite restaurant, Parks Edge in the Highlands. The BFF's chatted it up for an hour, sharing stories about family, work and dating, of course.

Summer didn't have much to share on the dating front except becoming more frustrated with having to wait to find Mr. Right. She joked, "Meagan, you're going to have to be my date if a good movie comes out because times are getting hard." That's when Meagan dropped a bombshell that would strain their friendship indefinitely. She looked Summer right in the eye and informed her that she was dating someone. In fact, she was dating Anthony. Summer congratulated her until the look in Meagan's eye signaled that was the wrong reaction. Meagan was referring to Summer's Anthony; her ex-boyfriend.

Summer laughed for a good five minutes thinking that her friend was playing the joke of the century. Meagan was a character and had developed quite the reputation as a comedian and prankster. There was only one problem with this prank, however. Meagan wasn't laughing and the cold, distant, evil look in her eye proved it. Meagan didn't utter a word. Instead, opting to hand Summer a digital camera which contained pictures of the couple hanging out at various parts of the city.

Summer could not believe her eyes. It was like a hailstorm suddenly erased a beautiful day at the beach. Anthony was Summer's boyfriend of two years who allowed his jealous ways to ruin their promising relationship. The relationship ended when he openly accused Summer of flirting with other men while he was away on business. He publicly berated, questioned and disrespected her while at a pool party the two hosted for all of their friends. Making matters worse, Anthony's friends had to calm him down and convince him that he was wrong because they all knew Summer was incapable of such behavior. Despite their efforts, he continued to harass her until finally Summer had no choice but to leave the pool party she was co-hosting.

Meagan was the one who was her biggest defender and cursed Anthony for being an idiot and walked Summer home. The two stayed up all night trying to figure out what happened while enjoying a few spirits to ease the night. Not only was Summer hurt but she was angry and embarrassed. She knew she didn't deserve such treatment from Anthony or any man because she has always been faithful in every relationship she entered.

Additionally, she was not a messy woman and opted for keeping her personal business private since her career in sales consistently placed her in the eye of the general public. Anthony later apologized and blamed his jealous, rageful fit on alcohol and stress but Summer declined to accept and left him for good. Suddenly recalling the incident in her head like it was yesterday, Summer asked, "Meagan, have you lost your damn mind?" "Why would you do that to me?"

With the calm of a cucumber, Meagan responded, "Listen Summer we are not getting any younger and Anthony expressed an interest in me one night while I was out with my girls. At first, I didn't pay him any mind because I figured that he was trying to get back with you but then I caught feelings for him. He loves me now. What's the big deal anyway? You said that you didn't want him anymore and it has been almost two years."

With tears in her eyes Summer responded, "Meagan, that's not the point. We are supposed to be best friends and dating each other's' ex-boyfriends is a violation of trust. I would never do that to you in a million years."

Meagan, now on the defensive, exploded. "How dare you judge me, you little Ms. Goody Two Shoes! I didn't have to tell you but I figured that you would be a grown woman about the situation. How about at least acting like my best friend and being happy for me?"

Summer interrupted, "I cannot believe that you have the nerve to fix your lips to ask me to be happy for you. Be happy for what? The fact, that you go behind my back to date my sloppy seconds because you can't find a man of your own. Get real."

Meagan was hurt. She smiled, stood up and took the shot heard round the world, "Summer, how about you stop being bitter?" "Bitter about what", Summer responded with a miffed smirk on her face. "Don't act Summer...you're just bitter about being the last one in the crew not to be in a relationship, so beat up on yourself, Old Maid, instead of me," and stormed out.

Summer sat, dazed about what had just taken place. The whole experience felt surreal. However, she was quickly adjusted back to reality when the server interrupted her to settle the bill. Summer looked up to alert Meagan that she needed to pay her half only to see her red Chevrolet Camaro speed off in the distance. "Great, she steals my ex and stiffs me for the bill all at the same time."

Instead of returning straight home, Summer ran some errands to try and distract herself from thinking about losing her best friend of ten years to of all people, Anthony. She felt betrayed, played, confused and stunned. Her strategy of visiting various places worked but she knew she would need an extended intervention for the long evening that awaited her. It was Saturday night too and she had no date in sight.

She needed some therapy and decided to visit her favorite spot, the bookstore. She decided to finally purchase a book that she kept hearing her girlfriends talk about changing their fortunes on the dating scene. She figured now was as good a time as ever and the night was quickly approaching.

The book was in short supply because the author did not release a lot of copies. However, she figured she would ask if it was in stock because she was overdue for some good news. She was in luck. Not only was the book in stock but it was on display as it was quickly generating a buzz. The display was beautiful and looked like a scene out of a wedding. His books were all gift-wrapped and placed on a table with white tablecloths. Summer quickly picked up a copy and headed for the house. It would serve as perfect company for the expensive bottle of wine she treated herself to earlier in the day.

Summer couldn't wait to start her evening and add some much needed distance from her morning. She poured a glass of Three Sisters Bukettraube, a rare South African wine, as she unwrapped the book that would entertain her for the evening. She couldn't help but marvel over the gift-wrapping because it was like nothing she had ever seen. She wondered who wrapped the books because the author was a man and there was definitely evidence of a woman's touch.

Further examination confirmed that her instincts were

right. The author credited Sandi Spells, the Paper Star, for the gift wrapping (www.sandispells.com). She was the celebrity wedding invitation sensation who recently did the invitations for Neyo's Cirque du Soleil Birthday Bash. Wow! She was really getting excited.

She took ten minutes to unwrap the book because she wanted to save the paper to keep because it was so beautiful. It was so intricate that she found herself amused with the challenge of actually opening it. She had already finished half a glass of wine before she finally peeled the last bow off. The book had been wrapped upside down but Summer didn't mind because the back cover revealed a picture of the author. She had to take a gulp of wine despite it not being proper etiquette because he was fine and had nice teeth!

His bio stated that he was a relationship expert but was single. As she nestled into her favorite loveseat she couldn't help but think, "What is a single man going to teach me about getting married? If he was such an expert, why wasn't he married himself? This should make for some very interesting reading indeed." Her friends were right, the book was good, the advice was the best she'd ever read and the stories were both funny yet powerful.

Summer found herself staying up all night to finish the book. It was like something was calling her to finish it. She simply could not put it down and turned each page with the anticipation that something big was going to happen. She enjoyed each chapter with two full glasses of wine and soft sounds of the radio which was tuned to V103 as her company for the evening.

As Summer read, she laughed, engaged in deep introspection but mostly she wondered, "Why isn't this man married?" Never before had she been more curious about the author than the actual content but if felt like both were connected in some strange way. As she finished the last page of the book, she smiled but was thirsty for more. She tried to watch television and even her favorite movie, *300*, but nothing worked. She, for some strange reason, could not get this author out of her mind. She decided to retire for the evening and recited her nightly prayer before preparing for bed. "God, grant me the serenity to accept the things I cannot change, the courage to change the things I can, and the wisdom to know the difference...and one more thing...A man!"

Summer laughed as she finished her prayer because she couldn't believe that she prayed for a man out loud. "Wow, that wine must have had something special in it because I'm losing my mind," she joked. Summer laughed it off and began to roll up her hair for the morning. Suddenly, something caught her attention and she immediately turned up the radio. "This cannot be real," she thought. The author of the book she just finished was going to be the late night guest for V103's weekly radio show, *The Quiet Storm with Joyce Littel.* Summer suddenly was no longer sleepy. In fact, she was rather perky in more ways than one.

Summer was excited and could not wait to hear what this doctor of love had to say. Joyce Littel was a legend and certainly pulled no punches when it came to asking the questions that all listeners wanted to know and, as usual, she didn't disappoint. "Dr. Love, I'll be honest, I have not read your entire book yet but the chapter titles alone had me in stitches. However, before we even talk about the book I want to know one thing...Why in the *hell* are you not married?

You are fine, smart, talented, single and have such a love and understanding of women. What gives?" Before he could answer Joyce took the liberty to tease her audience as all legendary radio host do. "Ladies, I will put the Doc on the hot seat and make him answer that question...when we return. You better not touch that dial!"

Summer laughed because Joyce was a fool! Summer was a nighthawk like her mother and could not resist calling her to listen to the *Quiet Storm*. She quickly filled her mom in on the details of reading the book and being surprised to hear the author on the radio. Her mother laughed and joked, "I can't wait to hear this; maybe if he has some sense I'll drop you off at the station. Lord knows you need a man."

"Very funny mom," Summer replied. "Shouldn't you be worried about your own man...where's father?" "Oh don't play Summer, your daddy is right where he always is- next to me in the very same bed that created you and your sisters," her mother snapped. "Ewww mom, I'm going to have to call you back on that one- goodnight mom." "Goodnight honey," her mother replied with her father's echo in the background.

The intro music for show began to play, *Soft and warm, the Quiet Storm with V 1-0-3,* and Joyce Littel was back in action. As promised, she asked Dr. Love the question all women wanted to know. Why is an attractive, God-fearing, tall, funny, attractive man who writes books telling women how to find love and get married not married himself? Dr. Love's answer shocked both Joyce and Summer. "Well, Joyce, the truth is that I have been waiting on God to send me the right one for quite some time now."

Joyce couldn't contain herself, "You mean with all the fine, talented, single, educated and man-loving women in Atlanta, *you* can't find one?" "Nope, it's actually harder than you think. Now, don't get me wrong, I can find lots of eye candy, sassy business suits and excellent cooks but I've found that finding the *one* woman, that perfect complement for me, to be quite elusive. Why do you think I wrote this book Joyce?"

Joyce was not buying it for one New York minute. "Dr. Love, oh you are too smooth but you are smart because you have women all over the city racing out to read this book now." Dr. Love seemed annoyed and caught off guard, "No Joyce, I'm dead serious. Do you think being 35 and single is something that any man would want? I've had my share of women, all the sex a man could imagine and still I'm lacking the one thing that matters most: A woman to share the rest of my life with."

Joyce laughed for a good five minutes and in classic radio host style, immediately opened up the phone lines and announced impromptu contest to *Date Doctor Love.* "Doc, you came to the right place tonight baby because I'm going to have you hooked up by midnight and it's already 11:55pm. This is going to be like taking candy from a baby. Ladies, your fingers BETTER start dialing right now....Hot Potato, Hot Potato."

Summer was laughing too but there was no way on God's green Earth that she was going to call the radio station. She thought, "This doctor might be cute but there is no way I am going to call into a station for any man...unless it's Common, Idris Elba, or Brad Pitt." Summer was sleepy and reached to turn off the radio but before she could, Doctor Love said something that completely blew her mind.

"Joyce," he replied, "You can hold all the contest you want but God has already told me where my woman is right now." Joyce queried, "Oh, is that so, then do tell." "Joyce, I know it sounds weird but God told me that the woman who would steal my heart has *already* read my book and is at home praying for me right now."

Summer literally fell out of her bed. This was too much of a coincidence. The more she listened, the more she realized that this man might actually be telling the truth. His reasoning for not having a woman in his life made so much sense once he explained it. She had never heard a man be so authentic, unguarded and transparent. He talked openly about the qualities that he was looking for in a woman and how he was more concerned with fit versus finding someone who is perfect. What shocked her was his admission that God had humbled him.

The Doc stated that, for many years, he thought that he could just pick a wife when he was ready but failed miserably. He talked about getting into a series of short-term relationships and breaking up because he realized that they were not the one. He indicated how these relationships were actually stressful because he had no tangible reason for really breaking up with the women. They simply were not the *one.* He talked about how much it hurt to break up with women who were absolutely phenomenal but how he refused to settle for anything less that the *one*.

When Joyce tried to query him on what these women did wrong his answer was simple yet powerful. "Joyce, the answer is *Nothing*. They are some of the most attractive, smartest, funniest, confident, God-fearing and caring women I've ever met. I refuse to make up something that is wrong with them because it would be a lie. That's why I have decided not to pursue another woman without God's blessing. I dislike being a heartbreaker because these women are my friends and great people. Privately, I wish that I would have never met them to hurt them but, then again, I would have never known if they were my true love or not."

"What man says stuff like that," Summer thought, "he sounds really frustrated yet hopeful?" Doc went on to explain the qualities that he wanted in the *one* and how he would allow God to position this woman in his life. He stated, "When God gives me the signal, then she won't have to do a thing because I have been waiting to court her my entire life." Literally, two seconds after he said that the lines at V103 lit up like a Christmas tree.

Every woman's question was the exact same, "Doctor Love, this is what drives us women crazy...can you *please* explain what you are looking for? That way we know whether to apply or not and can save ourselves a lot of heartache. By the way, I'm 5'5 with brown eyes, a nice shape and can make a mean apple tart if you like Doctor *Love*," the caller laughed as she hung up.

Doctor Love found the phone call amusing too and played right along. "Joyce, I do love dessert but my favorite is actually sweet potato soufflé. The woman who can make one even half as good as my mama will have me for life." The callers wouldn't let Doc off the hook and demanded that he produce his *list* for the *one*. Doc obliged but prefaced his answer as such, "Listen, this is just *my* list and while I'm sure a lot of men would agree, there will be variance because every man has different tastes. All of you are beautiful and deserve a great man because Lord knows we need you."

"Ladies, here we go- I could talk about this all night, especially over a little Musiq Soul Child in the background." Joyce cued up the music to his latest hit *So Beautiful* and Summer went mad. She slammed her hand on the pillow on her lap because that was *her* song. The Doc read, I call this list *"The 31"* because the woman who possesses all these thirty-one qualities will be my *ONE*:

31 Qualities of the One

1) She is self-sufficient but not independent.
2) She is emotionally strong yet vulnerable.
3) She doesn't pursue me but lets me know that she's interested.
4) She is mysterious yet honest.
5) She leaves me waiting yet is excited to see me each time.
6) She places high value on herself but is not conceded.
7) She takes excellent care of her body but is not superficial.
8) She is passionate about life, not just about me.
9) She wants to submit to a man but requires that I submit to God first.
10) She never lets me see her sweat and is able to express her true feelings calmly and clearly.
11) She remains in control and sets her own pace yet responds well to mine.
12) She expects to be respected and never has to ask for or demand it.
13) She is an excellent cook (or is willing to learn) and loves to cater to men but is very deliberate about who and when she does. It must be earned.

14) She is conservative yet willing to be exclusively wild with me once I've courted her appropriately and, therefore, deserve it.
15) She is confident enough to compliment other women and does not associate with messy ones.
16) She has high standards but is not judgmental.
17) She allows me to be the captain of the ship but naturally assumes the role of navigator.
18) She is a little bit bossy but does not get mad when I want to do a few things my way.
19) She is slightly possessive and does not like the idea of other women cooking for me.
20) She prefers prayer over arguing.
21) She likes hanging out with my parents, family and invites me to do the same with hers.
22) She's sexy but chooses to display it in a sundress versus a miniskirt.
23) She enjoys nature but is also prissy and likes to dress up.
24) She has the same positive attitude whether we vacation at the Holiday Inn or the Four Seasons.
25) She is intelligent but desires not to upstage her man.
26) She is the mother hen of her girlfriends not the gossiper.
27) She respects both of our parents and seeks their advice about how to handle me before a conflict arises.
28) She enjoys hooking my boys up with her girls.
29) She likes the finer things in life yet is frugal.
30) She wants to take care of our parents when they get old together.
31) She wants children or she wants children, non-negotiable.

By the time Doc finished his list, the studio was quiet enough to hear a pin drop. The female production assistants mouths were open and the men in the room worked quietly without saying a word while they high-fived. The lines that had been lit up constantly all night suddenly were empty and the callers dropped the line one by one. All was silent because the truth had been told: A man's list for his wife is only designed to fit ONE woman.

Although Dr. Love was in downtown Atlanta, if felt like the entire nation was in shock. Joyce broke the silence, "Wow, Doc you just shut a million listeners up but to be honest with you...I fit ALL those qualities baby. Boy, you better be lucky that I am already married to the baddest man on the planet or I would rock your little world inside out, through and through until it ain't no mo'! Can I get an Amen?!"

Doc couldn't help but laugh because Joyce Littel was a fool in a righteous sister-girl sort of way, which is why her radio show was the #1 show in all the land. "Joyce, now you see what I mean. Finding the one is difficult for men as well. We just don't believe in settling because many of us have been raised by women that fit many if not all of those qualities. We would rather remain serial daters and single indefinitely than settle for less than what we want in a wife."

The conversation turned serious, "Doc, do you think that you'll ever find her?" Now Doc responded like an author would, "Wouldn't you like to know...I guess the listeners will have to visit my website www.ringformula.com to find out." Joyce laughed, "Now that's the Dr. Love that I've grown to know and love."

"Ladies, you can also check him out on his Facebook page which already has close to 5,000 fans already but it's worth a try. Thank you Dr. Love for being our guest on Love & Relationships at V103, I'm your host Joyce Little, enjoy your evening and tune in next week for the sixty-two qualities that women want in a man. We'll show Dr. Love a thing or two ladies."

Joyce, adjusted her microphone and joked with Doc out loud as the show wrapped, "Boy, don't no woman want to take care of your mama." Doc laughed and got in one final comment before the show went off, "Yes she does and she's listening right now." Joyce quipped, "Yeah, we'll see how that works out for you" as the show went to commercial break.

A WOMAN'S QUEST FOR LOVE

Part Two:
"F.L.I.R.T. TO GET WHAT YOU WANT"

"Opportunity finds those who are unafraid to search for and take advantage of it." Meanwhile, Summer was wide awake having completely shaken off the effects of the South African wine. This man had just described her to a T. Making matters worse, her cell phone began buzzing like crazy. First were her mother and grandmother. What were they doing up? She knew the answer already because the women in her family were notorious for being nighthawks.

Her mother and grandmother were on the phone together since Summer's mom currently cared for her mother. "Summer, baby, we think you might have just found yourself a husband. If we didn't know better we would have thought that boy was looking right at you." Summer couldn't help but blush and told her mother and grandmother to go to bed.

Next was her high school friend Lisa who was calling all the way from New York. She was listening to the show on the internet. "Summer, girl, you know I rarely listen to the radio on the internet but I was up on Facebook and all these feeds kept referencing this Doctor Love guy interview on V103 so I tuned in. Summer, I swear that this man was describing you. He had this list of 31 qualities of the woman he wanted to marry and every last one of them fit you, except one. We all know you *ain't* frugal."

The old friends laughed and Summer admitted that she was listening too and needed some help in the frugal department. "What a yucky word," she thought. Her phone beeped again. "Lisa, girl, this is Anthony- remind me to fill you in when we speak again…you won't believe what happened to me today." Anthony, have you lost your everlasting mind calling me this late?"

Anthony interrupted, "Summer, let me apologize. I heard that Meagan went off on you today." Bitter with contempt yet still prideful, Summer responded as such, "Anthony, it really doesn't matter at this point because I have moved on." "I know", Anthony responded, "that's why I'm calling this late…just hear me out for a second, please?"

"This is going to sound funny but I was listening to V103 a few minutes ago and there was this corny love doctor on there. I'm playing, he actually made a lot of sense. He listed the 31 qualities that most men look for in a woman and I realized that you met almost every one of them. Listen, I was a fool to do wrong. I was immature, stupid and crazy and because of it I let the best thing that ever happened to me walk in and out of my life. I'm sorry."

Summer couldn't take it anymore, "Anthony, you haven't changed a bit. You are sorry but you date my best friend?" "Summer, you're right but you gave me no choice." "Excuse me", Summer replied. "You wouldn't return my phone calls, Facebook messages, emails or personal letters so I had to do something to get your attention."

Summer shook her head in disgust and then responded with the poise she was known for in the business world. She grabbed a digital tape recorder and asked Anthony to repeat himself. "Okay, Anthony, this is a lot for me to grasp, slow down and run that by me again to make sure I'm hearing this correctly." On cue, Anthony obliged and repeated the same words verbatim, obviously unaware that Summer was recording the conversation. Summer ended the conversation by indicating that she was tired and needed to sleep on his words and would call him later in the week and two hung up.

Summer laid awake in bed for hours trying to figure out her next move. Should she tell Meagan what Anthony was up to or let her find out for herself since she stabbed her in the back? Summer prayed about it and decided to do what made her sleep easiest at night. She knew that Meagan wouldn't believe her if she called so she decided to send the recording to her via letter and let Meagan make the next move. "What a mess", she sighed and finally called it a night. "Tomorrow has to be better than today."

Summer must have been a prophet because her luck changed as soon as she woke up. She checked her Facebook account like she did every morning and could not believe her eyes. Right there in her inbox, was a Facebook friend request and personal message from none other than Dr. Love himself.

It read, "I know this sounds weird but three of my friends suggested that we meet...according to them you have all 31 qualities that I'm looking for in a woman and then some. I would love to interview you if you are interested. By the way, you are very attractive." Summer was thrilled with excitement but resisted the urge to respond. She immediately picked up the phone and called the two women who gave the best dating advice in the world: Mom and Grandma.

"Hey mom, how are you?" Summer queried at 7:30 Saturday morning. "Summer, what's wrong. You only call this early if something if something is wrong." "Oh nothing, I just wanted to see what you and Grandma were doing." "Summer, you know your grandmother and I don't get up on the weekends before 9:30. What's wrong?" "It's nothing serious, guess who contacted me?" "It better be President Barack Obama calling me at this hour." Summer responded, "Not exactly but he is intelligent." "Well, who then Summer?" Summer smiled as she responded, "Dr. Love sent me a Facebook friend request."

Her mother rose up in the bed highly amused with the tone in her daughter's voice. "Well of course he did Summer. Your grandmother and I sent him an email after the show last night and told him how to contact you." Summer exploded in disbelief, "Mom, how could you do that to me...that is so embarrassing." Her mother enjoyed the moment, "Well, Summer we are not getting any younger and we would like to have some grandkids before we die you know."

Shocked, Summer went silent and stared at the phone in disbelief. Were these the same women who taught her to never tip her hand when it came to dating...be a lady...let the man pursue you?" She could not believe her ears and was truly at a loss for words. Finally, after enjoyed a prolonged laugh, her mother let her off of the hook. "Summer, I was only joking...that's what you get for calling me so early."

"Why don't you come over for lunch today so that you can tell your grandmother and we can talk. That will make your dad happy. He's been asking for some of your special salmon croquettes and I don't feel like cooking anyway. Your grandmother thinks she is a teenager and kept me up until half the night talking and dancing to the radio." Summer sighed in relief, "Mom, I was going to kill you and grandma. Tell father that I will cook for only him since he is the only one who loves me." "Keep that tone and you might end up cooking for the week," her mother quipped. See you around 3:00, okay?" "Okay mom, thanks."

Summer dropped by the Farmer's Market to pick up some ingredients for her special dish. She liked cooking, especially for her father who always raved about her cooking and made her feel like a princess. She was about to check out when her grandmother called and asked her to pick up some pork chops. "Grandmother, you know I don't cook that stuff and the doctors told you to lay off the pork."

Her grandmother laughed, "Summer, I wasn't talking about me. Your mother said that you were bringing a boy by here for us to meet so I figured you better pick up something in case he doesn't like seafood." Summer loved her grandmother's humor, "You and mom have jokes I see. Just make sure you have some good advice me." "Of course darling, don't we always? However, you can pick up some of those cashews I love for me and some Bear Claws for your mother."

Summer added some cashews and chocolate Bear Claws to her cart, checked out and headed to her parents house. As always, her father greeted her with a huge bear hug and surveyed her grocery bags as he carried them into the house in search of the evening's dinner. Summer closed the bags and told her dad that it was a surprise. Her dad smiled and winked his eye, "I hope that surprise has some salmon in it." Summer's mother interrupted, "Summer, don't mind your father, he is losing his mind...come on into this kitchen. Your grandmother and I are waiting on you." Father walked back upstairs with one final remark, "Call me when the salmon is ready."

Grandmother, mother and Summer unloaded the groceries together and exchanged small talk and compliments. "Mom, I love that blouse, did dad buy that for you?" They all laughed because everyone knew that father hated shopping and would avoid it at all cost. Summer and her mother began to chop up vegetables in preparation for the evening meal while her grandmother headed for the Bear Claws. As she dipped her hand in the bag, grandmother joked, "So, Summer, I hear that the Love Doctor wants some of your chocolate."

Summer's mother slapped grandmother's hand for her fast remark and dipping into the dessert before the meal. Summer laughed as her grandmother and mother passed licks until grandmother finally dropped the Bear Claw.

"Ladies, I didn't come over here to see you fight. I thought you had some advice for me." She filled mom and grandmother in on what she knew and showed them Dr. Love's Facebook profile for them to review. "Oh, he is cute, a

Christian, doesn't have a lot of pictures with random women, good hair...yeah he might be our future son-in-law if you play your cards right", her mother joked.

"So what should I do?", Summer asked. "Play it cool", her mother and grandmother said in unison. "He will pursue you but you'll have to keep him guessing to peak his interest. Men love mysterious women they cannot easily figure out. Simply respond to his interview request with a simple '*thanks*' and watch what happens."

Summer responded just as instructed and finished preparing a meal fit for a king. Her father enjoyed the meal as evidenced by getting a second helping and sporting a smile a mile long. He thanked her for the meal and peered down at her. "Who's this guy you're interested in?" Summer smiled and let her mother come to her defense. "Don't you worry about it, we already scoped him out and he meets your criteria", her mother snickered.

"I'll be the judge of that...when can I meet him?" "Father, he hasn't even asked me out yet and I may not like him." Her grandmother interrupted, "I don't know about that Summer, he sent you a message on this computer screen." Summer jumped back over the computer as she realized that she never logged out. "Grandma, get out of my business...let me see what you are talking about." Sure enough, Doc had asked her to dinner the following Saturday night to discuss the interview in more detail.

Doc had either really good taste or was incredibly lucky because he recommended her favorite restaurant, Park's Edge, which, ironically, was the same restaurant her friendship ended with Meagan. Summer was delighted but didn't want to come across as too easy. Her dad got into the action and reviewed the profile himself. He wondered, "What kind of Love Doctor has no love interests?" He was naturally very protective and wanted to make sure that no one was going to hurt his little princess.

He advised Summer to respond with a scheduling conflict to see how Doc would respond. Doc passed her father's test by changing the date to Friday night. Her father smiled, "He must really like you because he cancelled his Friday plans to meet you." Summer laughed and told her father that he better not try to embarrass her by *conveniently* showing up at her house to fix something fifteen minutes before the date.

A week went by and the excitement of Friday filled the air. Doc texted her earlier in the day to make sure that the plans hadn't changed. Even though it was just a first date with a complete stranger, Summer felt like she would have a great time. There was a certain electricity in the air. Always conscious of presenting her best, she took half the day off to get her hair and nails done. She even bought a new dress from Tootsies. She enjoyed some soft music as she prepared for her date.

Before she could even warm the curling iron, her routine was interrupted by a ring at the doorbell. "It's only 7:00, I know this man has not arrived an hour early." She scrambled to clothe herself and scanned the parking lot from her bedroom to see if it was him." One look and she knew exactly who it was at her door. She ran downstairs with a puzzled look on her face and opened the door.

"Hi dad, may I help you?", as she smiled. In his hands were some new door locks. Summer had been complaining about the current ones sticking all the time. "Hey baby girl, I just thought I would install these locks since I'm off of work today. Why are you so dressed up...going on a date?" He could hardly control his grin and immediately started examining the locks.

"You think you're slick father...I know your game", Summer smirked as she placed her hands on her hips. "What? I am just replacing your locks...it should only take an hour...don't mind me." Summer laughed as she bounced back up the steps. Playfully, she wondered if she should text Doc to give him a heads up about her father. She decided against it, opting to see how Doc worked under pressure.

Doc arrived fifteen minutes early but decided to remain in his car until the exact time. At exactly 8:00 sharp, he collected the flowers he picked up for Summer and reached to ring her doorbell. However, before his finger could reach the bell, Summer's father opened the door to ensure that the locks were working properly. Both men were startled and gave each other an inquisitive stare.

Doc extended his hand and introduced himself, "Hi, I'm Doc." "Hello, I am Summer's father. Know anything about installing locks?" Immediately put on the spot but recognizing the importance of making a good impression, Doc lied. "Sure, what do you need me to do, sir?" Her father smiled, "I need you to put this one on the basement door while I secure this one."

Doc was put on the spot and his face showed it by turning as red as the roses in his hand. "Doc, you can put your flowers on the table and let my daughter know that you are here." Doc then ran up the steps of the condo and placed the flowers on the table and waved as Summer as she finished styling her hair in the bathroom. She smiled and seemed to be enjoying this little test.

Doc was also amused and actively conjuring up a plan for pretending like he was an expert at installing locks. He ran to his car to grab his toolset and got down to work. Immediately, the questions started from her dad. "What are your intentions with my daughter", her father queried with the glare of a gladiator." Doc responded, "To be honest sir, this is the first date. I really just want to get to know her and enjoy a nice dinner."

Doc fiddled with the locks and answered her father's questions one by one. He was surprised how quickly he was able to assemble the locks without prior experience. However, there was one last part he could not figure out. It seemed so simple but Doc didn't want to delay the dinner and figured that he would fare better asking for direction versus playing dumb. "Sir, I have been trying to figure this thing out for ten minutes now. How do you get to this pin?"

Her father took the plastic off and laughed, "Rookie operation, son?" "Doc laughed and peered at the handyman work of her father, "Well, that was the only the part I couldn't figure out. The lock is almost done and mine is actually right side up." The two men laughed and helped each other complete the job. Finally, her dad wished Doc good luck and was on his way after getting a hug from his daughter.

After closing the door, Summer let out a sigh and apologized for her dad. "I had no idea he was coming over here; he just showed up. I was going to tell you but I wanted to have a little fun with you." "Well, turnabout is fair play. The next date will be at my family reunion. We'll see how you like that." They shared a laugh and then Doc's tone changed as he finally had an opportunity to appreciate Summer's beauty. "Wow, you look amazing. I can see why your daddy guards you like Fort Knox."

"Thanks, you don't look half bad yourself but you'll need to wash your hands before you dine with me." Forgetting all about dinner, Doc apologized. "We may need to change the plans. The reservations were for 8:30 and didn't anticipate installing locks." Summer smiled, "Go wash your hands... I pushed the reservation back to 9:15 since you two were bonding."

Doc and Summer enjoyed the best dinner, starting with the appetizers. Doc and Summer enjoyed the best dinner starting with an order of Crispy Calamari drizzled with chili sauce and wasabi aioli and Five Spiced Seared Scallops accompanied by edamame and spicy ginger sauce. For the main course, Doc ordered the Grilled Lamb Bone Chops with parmesan reggiano risotto and tangine sauce while Summer enjoyed the Pan Seared Seabass with Yukon truffle mashed potatoes, asparagus chipotle cream sauce.

Better than the meal, however, was the conversation and electric chemistry they shared. Doc listened to funny stories about Summer's dad scaring off her ex-boyfriends and Summer laughed as Doc talked about the elderly women who tried to hit on him when he spoke at churches.

After dinner, the two shared dessert and a bottle of Riesling and then the conversation turned serious. Summer inquired as to why Doc had never been married before. His answer shocked and worried Summer. "Honestly, I get bored easily. Sometimes, I can be totally head over heels for someone and then lose interest. It's frustrating because I do wish to settle down and begin a family."

Doc stared off into space as Summer concocted a plan. Thanks to mom and good old grandma, she had just the remedy to keep Doc's interest for a lifetime. Time to initiate Operation F.L.I.R.T. Summer wasted no time. "Doc, thanks for dinner. How did you know this was my favorite restaurant?"

Initially Doc played dumb and then spilled the beans. "You posted something on your Facebook about this place being your favorite restaurant." "I see", Summer replied. "Well, it's been a very long time since I have been treated so well and enjoyed such stimulating and interesting conversation. You are a great listener and I do appreciate the fact that you took time to plan something special for me. Doc, will you excuse me for a minute?" "Sure", Doc responded and stood up and pulled out her chair like a gentleman. As Summer walked to the bathroom Doc silently prayed, "Lord please don't let me lose interest...I really like her."

The server returned with the check that Doc paid with no reservations. The conversation, the company and the chemistry made the price of the meal insignificant. As he signed the bill, the server asked him for his valet ticket. Doc found it a little odd not to present the ticket outside but didn't hesitate to give it to her. Suddenly, Doc looked at his watch. Summer had been gone for close to fifteen minutes.

He wondered what was going on. Was she sick, did she leave, should he ask one of the waitresses to check on her? Immediately, he headed toward the bathroom but was stopped by their server. "Excuse me sir, your date asked if you could meet her outside?" Puzzled, Doc headed for the exit. He opened the door and Summer was right there waiting for him.

The valet had already pulled his car around and Summer was standing there motioning for him to come closer. Doc paused for a moment appreciating the picturesque moment of Summer's elegance, smile and beauty. As he approached, she leaned in close and whispered in his ear, "I have some plans for you as well. Let's get out of here." Amused, Doc questioned, "Where are we going." Summer's answer intrigued Doc, "Stop asking so many questions and just drive until I tell you to stop. Let's go have some **FUN**."

The two hopped in the car with Summer giving directions without revealing a specific destination. They drove for about twenty minutes and when they finally arrived, Doc looked puzzled. "Where are we? We are in the middle of nowhere." "You scared?" Summer responded with a challenging tone. Doc smiled, "No, I just wasn't sure if I needed to bring my gun or my knife," he responded with machismo. Summer played along and grabbed on to his biceps **(TOUCH)**, "Bring the guns?"

Doc didn't say a word but he was thoroughly intrigued despite being a little nervous. They walked around to the side of an industrial building where a neon sign reading *595 Lounge* hung. The bouncer greeted Summer like a sister and pounded Doc up like he was a teammate and then proceeded to frisk him aggressively. "Hey man, you better treat my little sis right… have a good time", the bouncer warned and then opened up the door. Immediately, the soulful sounds of a female crooner filled the crisp nighttime air. Summer smiled, grabbed Doc's hand and led him to the front row that was already reserved for them.

The live band was already into the beginning of their second set and the crowd was at a fever pitch. Finally, Doc realized what the surprise was. His favorite band, *Soul Factor,* was playing with lead singer Stephanie Parker, aka Spark. He glanced at Summer while she admired Spark's heels and how she was able to jump and dance around in them like they were flats. "You go girl", Summer shouted from her seat.

Immediately, the band stopped the song and focused their attention on the front row. "Hold up, hold up, hold up *595 Lounge*...No, you didn't bring this fine man up in here on your arm like that Summer!" Spark looked directly at Doc while the band had fun playing the theme music from the game show Jeopardy. Spark laughed, winked at the band and then hopped off stage and sat down right next to Doc. Doc's heart was beating a mile a minute and Summer's placed her hand over her mouth because she couldn't believe what Spark was about to do.

Spark's tone changed to a low, melodic bedroom volume and she asked, "So Doc, what say you?" Doc's eyed popped out of the back of his head as he tried to think of a response. Spark had fun with him, "Come on Doc, I'm sure you have something to say", and then cued the band to stop the music so that it was dead quiet. Everyone in the place smiled with a look of anticipation. It was like everyone knew what was about to happen but Doc himself. Startled yet composed, he gathered himself to say, "Well, I'm glad to be", but before he could say "here", Spark grabbed the microphone and began singing the classic hit, *Tell Me Something Good.*

Spark jumped back on stage and winked at the couple and continued to entertain the crowd to the classic that made everyone sing. In unison the audience sang, "Tell me something good, tell me that you love me, oh, baby, baby, baby, baby!" Doc and Summer joined in while waving their hands side to side. Doc smiled all night as he and Summer sang along with every hit that Soul Factor and Stephanie

Parker played.

They even danced when the band went up-tempo and ran through the lounge making everyone get up by taking their chairs away. Doc danced until sweat dripped down his face trying to keep up the energetic, rhythmic moves of Summer. The two shut the *595 Lounge* down and finally headed home.

On the way to the car, Doc placed his arm around Summer and asked the question that had been running through his mind most of the evening. "Did you already know that I love live music and that *Soul Factor* is one of my favorite bands of all time?" Summer blushed, "Doc, of course I did...you're not the only one who does their research." Doc was baffled, "How did you find that out?" I saw it on your Facebook page and saw the CD sitting on your dash in the car. Doc's interest was piqued, "So, when did you plan this?"

"Sweetheart, that's why I was in the bathroom so long ... I was checking with my girl, Spark, to see if they were performing tonight. We met at the gym a few months ago and I had been promising her that I would come out and support. She put us on the list and she warned me that she was going to test you. That's why I was laughing when she sat next to you. I thought she was just playing and couldn't believe that she was that silly."

Doc smiled and peered right into Summer's eyes, "Well, thank you. I haven't had that much **FUN** on a date in a very, very long time." Summer cut her eyes at Doc. "I mean ever", he responded. Doc pulled up to Summer's house and thanked Summer for a wonderful evening and went in for a kiss. He was met with Summer's soft finger, "Doc, I don't kiss on the first date but I had a great time." Doc was shocked. What went wrong? They had a great dinner, great conversation, sang and danced; he just didn't get it. Summer smiled as if she could read his thoughts.

"Doc, I had an awesome time but I'm a lady. I treat those who are special to me special as well. However, I don't just kiss guys just because we had an awesome date. Kissing is special to me and I must really know a man before I share any part of my mouth with him.

You did well for your first date but you have a lot more work to do to come close to these", as she freshened her lip gloss and rubbed her soft lips together. "Besides, Doc, I don't have to," as she began to open her door. Doc immediately jumped out and opened her door.

Frustrated yet in full respect of her views Doc asked, "Well, can I at least have a hug?" "Sure", Summer responded and opened her arms. As they hugged, Summer figured that she would have a little fun with him and placed her hands on the back of his neck. "Okay girl, you are playing with fire", Doc warned. Summer inserted her key into her lock and flirtatiously replied, "I like a little fire...Goodnight Doc."

Doc burned with passion and **Intrigue** as he waited for Summer's door to close to make sure that she made it in safely. Even though he had just dropped Summer off, he already wanted to see her again. As Doc drove home listening to the sounds of *Soul Factor* in his car, he thanked God. "God, I think you might have picked the right one baby- no disrespect Lord." He couldn't help but marvel at everything that Summer brought to the table. She was sexy yet classy, hot yet conservative, quiet yet spontaneous, flirtatious yet held to her morals and convictions.

With the confidence of a man holding a million dollar lottery ticket, Doc declared Summer his girlfriend and future wife. He smiled as he pulled into his garage with his mind racing of all the ideas and ways to impress Summer to win her first kiss, love and life-long commitment. As he jumped into the shower with the energy of a hyperactive child, he noticed a text from Summer indicating that she had a wonderful time and that all was safe. He wondered whether or not he should text back or whether it would be too much. He laughed at himself and thought about how wonderful it was to feel anxious about dating again.

Doc contacted Summer two days later with the hopes of inviting her on another date. He purposely skipped a day to avoid appearing pressed and desperate. When he called Summer they spoke for hours. She was such an excellent listener and seemed genuinely interested in him. She asked him questions about his family, career ambitions, biggest fears, whether he felt he had truly blossomed into the man God intended for him to be and, if not, what he needed to work on to accomplish that.

Doc was blown away. Never before had a woman shown such a genuine interest in who he was as a person. Just when Doc thought things couldn't get any better, Summer asked the question that would forever make her uniquely special. "Doc, would you like any help?"

It was such a simple question but its effect was profound. "What do you mean?" Doc asked. "Do you need any help with becoming the man God intends for you to be?", Summer reemphasized. Summer spoke with such confidence that Doc couldn't do anything but be honest.

"Sure, I need all the help I can get to be honest." Summer spoke softly yet confidently,

"Well then, when you're ready, just tell me what you want me to do and I help as best I can."

Doc's mouth was wide open as he stared at the phone and whispered to himself, "Is this woman real?" Suddenly overwhelmed with emotion, all Doc could do was thank her and end the call.

Doc wondered where Summer had been all of his life. He had struggled for so long trying to do everything by himself that he honestly had forgotten what it felt like to have some help. That's when it dawned on him; God had sent him a helpmate. He was amazed at how Summer was able to be submissive by offering help without being critical or condescending. His recent dating experiences had conditioned him to expect criticism, a power struggle or someone appearing genuine only to position themselves around the city's movers and shakers. Summer was so **Loving**, selfless and sincere. It was like a dream.

Apparently, Doc's head was too far in the clouds because he forgot to ask Summer on a second date. He called her again and asked her to attend a musical play that was in town, *Twist*. Although he didn't show it, he was crestfallen when Summer informed him that she already had a full week of plans and that she would have to call him back because she was on the other line.

She was cordial and nice but was obviously preoccupied by something or someone else. Although he had no right, Doc was upset, jealous and couldn't stop thinking about what could possibly keep her busy all week. He started to ask but decided to play it cool to avoid coming across as possessive and needy. Immediately, he remembered why so many men tend to avoid getting emotionally involved while dating. "This woman is driving me crazy already and she's not even my girlfriend." He wished her good luck on a fabulous week and indicated that he would call her later.

Old habits die hard so Doc immediately went through his phone list and called a few women he had dated but never really gotten serious with to distract himself and boost his ego. However, five minutes into the conversation he found himself comparing them to Summer. He ended both phone calls quickly and decided to do a little research.

He went to Summer's Facebook page to see if she posted anything that might give him clues. As predicted, her status update read, "Busy week- art event on Monday, workout club on Tuesday, 30 Under 30 Award Luncheon Wednesday". It was true; Summer was committed to events all week.

Doc played it cool Monday and Tuesday. On Wednesday, he decided to do something bold. He was **intrigued** by Summer and how she had so many varied interests. His ego was a little bruised but it only led him to want to pursue and learn more about this mysteriously **interesting** woman. He wondered why she just didn't tell him about these events and ask him to attend. He googled the 30 Under 30 Awards and learned that she was being recognized as one of the recipients for being one of the thirty most influential women who was under thirty. Initially, he thought that he would just drop by but figured that it would be too obvious and give off a stalker vibe. Instead he called her early that morning.

"Summer, I'm going to be honest with you. I was looking at your status update on Facebook and noticed that you are attending an award ceremony tonight. How come you didn't tell me about it?" In a soft, playful voice she responded, "I guess you didn't ask."

"Well I'm asking now...are you getting an award?"

"Actually I am", she responded followed by a long, awkward silence.

"Well, are you going to tell me what you are winning...I may want to support, Doc jabbed playfully." "Really," Summer responded with a smile. "Well I am being honored for my work helping women to find health and balance in their lives."

Doc was amazed. Summer was like a sexy Mother Theresa and was so modest and humble. "Doc, I didn't tell you about it because I figured that you might be busy and my family will be there and you and my father..." Doc laughed as he interrupted, "Summer, I certainly understand...you don't have to say another word. Well, your family must be very proud. Congratulations". "Thank you, Doc."

Doc took the time to inquire about Summer's many interests, ambitions, and fears. He even asked about her favorite colors (purple and orange). The two stayed on the phone another two hours as Doc listened to Summer talk about her desire to improve the health of all women worldwide, help her parents live longer, repair the relationship with her best friend and develop into a woman that would make her grandmother proud.

Immediately, Doc sensed a tone of sadness in her voice. Instinctively, he asked, "Is your grandmother living?" "Oh God yes," Summer responded with relief. "She's alive and active but she's 89 and I know that her time will come. She's my best friend and I want to do everything in my power to make her proud while she is still living. That's not what I am sad about. I'm really hurt and disappointed that Meagan and I no longer speak after eight years of talking with each other almost daily." Summer told Doc the whole story about how they fell out and her desire to be close with Meagan again. She expressed a fear of losing the ones closest to her and how she felt powerless to change it.

Doc listened for as long as Summer needed and offered emotional support until it was time for both of them to go to work. Even though it was early morning and the sun was shining, Doc couldn't help but reflect on Summer's sadness about Meagan and her grandmother. He was honored that she had been so **Revealing** and trusted him enough to share such a personal and sensitive moment with him.

He wanted to help but didn't know how. If only he could do something to cheer her up. He dressed for work and hopped in his car. As soon as he pulled out the driveway, he saw a woman gardening. She had the biggest smile on her face as she admired her beautiful flowers. That was it! Doc would get Summer some flowers congratulating her on her award.

He called up a local florist, Rockland Florist, and ordered a breath taking arrangement of bright orange Gerbera daisies with purple mini carnations. He sent the flowers to her job with a special note. "I pray that this cheers you up for your big award today. Please share at least one daisy with grandma ... congrats, Doc."

Doc smiled and felt good about himself. He liked being helpful and prayed that his gift would be delivered on time and before the award ceremony. He arrived at work and was bombarded with responsibilities and completely forgot all about following up to see if the flowers had arrived. He glanced at his phone and noticed that he had missed the delivery confirmation from the florist. No more than five minutes passed when Summer called to thank him. With emotion in her voice she revealed, "Doc, this is the sweetest gift any man has ever given me- outside my dad that is. Thank you."

Doc couldn't help but toot his own horn and sell himself. After all, he was on a mission and Summer was the objective. "Well, Summer if you would tell me more about your varied interests and concerns, you might find yourself getting all the support you desire." Summer laughed and joked about Doc needing a lesson in modesty but the gift had deep impact on her...and her father. "Hold on Doc, someone wants to speak with you", and she handed the phone to her father.

"Doc, your flowers look almost as good as the ones I got Summer." Doc didn't know how to respond and opted for silence. "Ah Doc, I'm just playing with you son. You are my kind of guy." Summer grabbed the phone and informed Doc that she would call him back later; the family was celebrating and heading to dinner.

After speaking with Summer, Doc was on cloud nine. He got on his knees and thanked God for sending Summer into his life. At that moment, he asked God to show him the way to heart and to prepare him to be her future husband. He finally felt in control over his destiny. No longer did he have to search for Mrs. Right. Instead, he would focus all of his energy on making her happy for an eternity and securing her hand in marriage.

Doc called his parents and younger brother and spoke candidly with them about his feelings for Summer and received sound advice. His dad instructed him to give the relationship time and not to rush so that a foundation of friendship could be developed. However, his father advised him not to wait too long because "the good ones" don't tend to stick around and wait very long. His mother chimed in too, "Don't wait too long because I need some grandchildren." The family shared a laugh and Doc set course over the next year to make Summer his wife.

Doc and Summer dated for the next twelve months, making sure to improve the quality of their friendship and take the necessary time to truly learn and grow together. Doc spent more time at work preparing for the expenses of being a husband while Summer spoke with her parents, grandmother and married friends about what it took to be the best wife possible. At the end of twelve months, Doc counted up his cash and headed straight to Tiffany & Co. Jewelers to purchase a diamond ring.

He was unsure what style fit Summer best but knew that he would know the right one when he saw it. Needless to say, the process was more difficult than he thought. Despite doing his research prior to coming in, there were simply too many choices. He wandered around aimlessly for one hour when finally the sales represented insisted that she help him. After an hour of refusing help and getting nowhere, Doc sheepishly let his guard down.

The sales associate was cute and graciously agreed to help. She asked him a few questions to better assist him. "Describe what type of things your girlfriend likes, what type of perfume she wears, is she classy, trendy, conservative, Christian, tall, short, portly, slender...?" The questions made Doc even more nervous. However, Doc was on a mission and defeat was not an option. He asked the sales representative if there was a computer he could access to show her something. The two walked over to the computer and Doc pulled up his Facebook account and showed the rep Summer's profile.

The associate appeared startled and looked like she had seen a ghost. It was so obvious that Doc asked, "Excuse me, do you know her?"

"No sir, I thought I did- she favors my sister that's all." Immediately, the sales rep got up and told Doc to follow her. "Don't you need to see more than just her profile picture...there are some photo albums in here." "No, I know exactly what she wants...trust me on this one." She left and went to the back and came back with a beautiful princess cut diamond. Doc was skeptical and kept asking for more choices to compare and contrast to ensure that he picked the best selection.

The sales representative would not comply and repeated, "This is the ring sir...you'll just have to trust me." Doc wasn't buying it and was taken back by her boldness and refusal to even allow him to look at other rings. "No offense ma'am, I know you are the professional but I have never seen a ring that looks like that and I'm not sure she will like it. Can we go with something a little more traditional so that I am guaranteed not to go wrong?"

The sales representative smiled but refused again, "Listen, you'll just have to trust me...I know this type of woman and *this* is her ring." Doc's anxiety turned to anger and he asked for the manager so he could file a complaint. The manager spoke with the sales representative and came back over to Doc.

"Sir, I have to agree with my representative here...this is the ring you are looking for. We are so confident that she will love his ring that we are going to offer you an employee discount as a sign of good nature and customer service. If she does not love this ring, you can bring it back and get your full money back. However, we are confident that not only will she love it but she'll love *you* for picking out the ring of her dreams." Doc was overwhelmed and purchased the ring on the spot and thanked them for their help. On the way out he joked, "If I have to come back because she doesn't like it I'm going to sue you for ruining my life."

Doc planned the perfect evening and presented Summer with the diamond ring at dinner. When Doc got down on one knee, she began to cry in anticipation. When he opened the box, the normally reserved Summer exploded in excitement. He imagined that she would be excited but had no idea that she would respond like that. It was like he had performed a miracle. "How did you know about this ring? This is the ring I dreamed of my entire life. How did you find it? Only Tiffany & Co. carries this particular ring because it's so rare and so uniquely me."

She hugged Doc and formally accepted his hand in marriage. She was so happy, surprised and excited that Doc had miraculously found the ring of her dreams that she couldn't even eat the rest of her meal nor the celebratory, complimentary dessert. She stared at Doc and her ring the entire night and cried four times on the way home. "God is so, so good", she shared with Doc and kissed him on the lips.

A WOMAN'S QUEST FOR LOVE

PART THREE: *"HAVING IT ALL"*

"The Lord works in mysterious ways and his plan is always significantly better than our own." Summer couldn't wait to share her news and exuberantly began calling everyone she knew. However, her exuberance quickly turned to sadness because she realized that she couldn't share this moment with the one person who helped her dream about it for eight years, Meagan. Meagan was still in denial and hurt from receiving that package with Anthony's phone conversation from Summer and had cutoff all forms of communication. The two had not spoken with one another in almost a year.

Summer struggled about whether she should contact Meagan or just allow her to find out on her own. After praying about it, Summer did what most women would do...she called her mother. This was a delicate situation and her approach could either heal or further damage their strained relationship. Both her mother and grandmother advised her to extend the olive branch to Meagan and try to forgive her.

Summer agreed and called Meagan after twelve long months. "Hello?", Meagan answered annoyed. "Hi Meagan, this is Summer...we should talk." Meagan didn't respond well, "We have nothing to talk about it unless you are ready to apologize." Summer didn't feed in to the negative energy and took the initiative. "Meagan, we have been friends for nine years and I want to at least do my part to ensure that we make it ten. Can you come over to my house later today?" Reluctantly, Meagan accepted.

Meagan arrived at Summer's house prepared for a fight but hoping for resolution.. However, when she arrived she was pleasantly surprised and relieved to be greeted with a hug and sweet aroma of homemade muffins. Summer cut right the chase, "Meagan I have some very special news to share with you but first I want you to know that you are still my best friend and that I forgive you."

Meagan's pride kicked in even though she knew better, "Forgive me for what?" Summer handled her smoothly and sincerely, "For allowing us not to speak for an entire year- you are my best friend and I miss you." Meagan immediately began to cry and apologized for allowing a man to become between the two of them.

She confided in Summer about how Anthony played her and was now dating one of girls from her crew. She indicated that she wanted to call Summer and make up but was too embarrassed to do so. The two hugged and they enjoyed one another's company and many blueberry muffins again like nothing had ever happened.

When it came time to leave, Meagan inquired, "Summer what was the big news you had to share with me?" Summer had taken off her engagement ring prior to Meagan arriving to avoid conflict and give her an option in case the interaction went sour. Still cautious not to ruin a good thing and keep the focus on their rekindled relationship, Summer avoided the question.

"Oh, it was nothing big. I'll tell you later." Meagan grinned like she knew something and then asked Summer to walk her to the door to call an end to a great conversation with her best friend. As Meagan walked out of the door, she smiled and Summer and asked, "So you're really not going to tell me huh?" She could tell that Meagan wanted to tell her something but was struggling. Finally, she took matters into her own hands. "Summer, where's your ring?"

With a look of shock and bewilderment, Summer asked, "What do you mean?" Meagan smiled and grabbed Summer's left hand. "Where's your engagement ring?" Summer looked puzzled and couldn't help but ask, "Who told you?"

Meagan pulled her best friend outside and they sat next to each other on the steps. "Summer, I know that Doc proposed to you...you don't have to hide it." "How did you know...and how do you know Doc?", Summer asked with a look of amazement. "I met him last week", Meagan responded. "Oh really, how is that?", Summer queried.

"Well, a few months ago I broke it off with Anthony and took up a second job to fill my free time so I wouldn't go crazy. I decided to get a part time job at our favorite store, Tiffany & Co. Jewelers, since I already knew the inventory. So, I'm working one day and this guy walks in looking very handsome but extremely anxious. I ask him his name and how I could help him. He introduced himself as Doc and told me that he was dating this very special woman and wanted to select the perfect ring. Immediately, my antennas up because I got the funniest feeling that he was talking about you.

I asked him to describe you so I could pick out the perfect ring. He took it one step further and opened up his Facebook account so I could review your sense of style from your profile. Well, Summer, to make a long story short, when I saw him type in your name and your picture came up, I knew that God had smiled on me. I was looking for a way to make things up to you and praying that we would randomly meet in the store one day. I missed your friendship but had too much pride to just call out of the blue.

I figured one day you would revisit your favorite again. When Doc walked in, I knew exactly what God wanted me to do. I played it off like I didn't know you but insisted that I was 100% sure that you would love a particular ring. Girl, he gave me such a hard time because the ring was so unique that I had to tell the manager it was for you so he could authorize a company discount. Finally, Doc put down those other ugly rings and walked out with the one you are hiding upstairs.

"So, Summer, stop playing it cool and trying to protect my pride and show me what that wedding ring looks like on your finger!" Summer cried tears of joy, hugged Meagan and raced upstairs. She put on her ring and came back outside to show Meagan. "Bam!", she shouted as she displayed the ring they had both seen twenty times before but was now permanently on her wedding finger. The two friends screamed with excitement, hugged and cried tears of joy. Then suddenly, it clicked. Summer remembered Doc telling her a story about how the woman at the jewelry store was kind of bossy but seemed to know so much about her that he took her recommendation.

Summer was so overwhelmed with joy that all she could do was close her eyes and thank God for how good he had been to her through all of the trials and tribulations. Never in her wildest dreams could she imagine that God would lead Doc to Meagan so that she could have both her husband and best-friend in her life.

Looking back, Summer couldn't believe how her life changed in just twelve months. She went from being single with a best friend to finding a man but losing her best friend, to getting engaged and getting her best friend back. It was like a fairy tale ending to a very trying year. Now, she could look forward to marrying the man of her dreams and Meagan being her maid of honor.

I guess it goes to show that life is a journey and that you are almost assured of losing things in life along the way (money, friends, cars, relationships) but you should never lose your faith! While Meagan lost hers and made the unfortunate decision of betraying her best-friend and getting betrayed herself in the process, Summer relied on God and found the man of her dreams. Despite Meagan's betrayal, God listened to Summer's prayers and used Meagan to help Doc find the perfect ring to serve as lifelong evidence of the reward that maintaining faith in Him can yield.

Another important lesson is that Summer put her faith into action. She didn't just stay at home and hope and pray for God to send her a man. She put her faith into action and used F.L.I.R.T (Fun, Loving, Interesting/Intriguing, Revealing, Touching) to seize opportunities to attract a man and showcased her ability to be a lifetime helpmate and prized catch. The following scripture comes to mind to illustrate this point:

What good is it, my brothers, if someone says he has faith but does not have works? Can that faith save him? If a brother or sister is poorly clothed and lacking in daily food, and one of you says to them, "Go in peace, be warmed and filled," without giving them the things needed for the body, what is that? So also faith by itself, if it does not have works, is dead. But someone will say, "You have faith and I have works." Show me your faith apart from your works, and I will show you my faith by my works (James 2:14-18, *ESV).*

Summer put her faith into action and woke up each day open to new opportunities. She was hopeful and pursued the opportunity to befriend Doc to see if he was the man that God had designed to be her soul mate. Meagan, on the other hand, lost her faith and figured that her only chance at love was to steal it from another. Both women had equal chance at finding true love but their perspectives differed.

Summer knew first hand of the many benefits that a wife offers a husband. She grew up watching her mother care for her father and how much he struggled when she was out of town on business. Thus, she saw first-hand how much stronger men are when their wife is around. In stark contrast, Meagan's parents divorced when she was just a small child and witnessed her mother get involved with married men in desperation for love. Thus, she had no evidence of a woman adding value to a man outside of non-exclusive sex.

Regardless of their parental backgrounds, the truth is that God affords all of us the ability to choose to have faith or not. If you open your eyes to opportunities versus remaining lifetime skeptics then you can change your perspective. You can learn to enjoy the journey versus being stressed by it to the point that you make unwise, unhealthy and harmful decisions that further damage your psyche. Meagan saw the look of anxiety on Doc's face and how invested he was in pleasing her. She knew why Doc felt the way he did because her best friend was an amazing woman.

Meagan knew that Doc could search high and low and never find another woman as loving, caring, fun, interesting, intriguing and trusting as Summer. Thus, she knew that Doc's life would be instantly upgraded the minute he decided to marry Summer. Regardless of her lack of access to her own father, she saw firsthand of how much value a woman can add to a man.

Ladies, I hope this final chapter has provided more evidence that men, beyond a shadow of a doubt, desperately need and desire you. Doc, like so many single men in this world, was looking for lifetime companionship and struggled the same way that women do. He refused to settle for anything less than what God promised him despite how long it took and was growing restless. He decided to invest that restless energy in to writing about love, relationships and helping others find it; all the while, hoping that God would miraculously transform those works into finding a wife for himself. Faith without works is dead, right?

The moral of the story is that men, of all types and calibers are ready to meet and marry you. Please don't buy into the media hype that men do not want you and purposely opt for a lifetime of serial dating over marriage. It's simply untrue. Men just hide their needs a lot better than women do and tend to live by a warrior code that encourages them to not show emotion, need or desperation. Men are taught to be stoic and that too emotion is a sign of weakness and poor leadership.

However, peeling away the masculine façade will reveal men with the same emotional needs as you. Men desire companionship, lifetime friendship, commitment and family. They are searching for you even though their faces and actions may demonstrate otherwise. Men are different from women but have many of the same needs as women. Men do need you and are waiting to make your acquaintance so they can court and marry you if it's God's will.

I'll say it again, men do need you but they need you to do your part. You must be available, open minded and certain of your ability to be a great wife so that marriage minded men can find you. Men are focused when it comes to finding a wife. Their standards for a wife are significantly higher than they are for a girlfriend. After all, you can always break up with a girlfriend but a wife is supposed to last for a lifetime. If you possess self-doubt to the point that it renders you overly-skeptical, hostile, insecure and inactive (staying at home) then marriage minded men will ignore you in search of the *one* who is convinced of their self-worth and value.

Summer had that confidence and was active about giving men a chance to make her acquaintance. She possessed the proper mindset for attracting married minded men. She did not chase Doc but seized the opportunity to flirt with him. Next, her only action was to make her total package known and allow Doc to do the rest. Quite simply, she afforded Doc the opportunity to meet the woman of his dreams who could complete him for a lifetime.

Doc, was appreciative too because Summer's assertive yet classy flirtatiousness allowed him to solve a major dilemma: Seeking a wife but being unable to find the *one* person to make that a reality. There are millions of men just like Doc who wish to marry but need access to you. These men need you at your best so that you will have the confidence to flirt and allow them to pursue, court and marry you. It worked for Summer, it worked for your mother and grandmother and it will work for you!

I feel strongly that the primary reason that many marriage minded men and women remain single is lack of access to one another. I encourage both men and women to be more purposeful, hopeful and faithful in their quest for finding their better half. Ladies, don't sit home waiting on Boaz to knock on your door; position yourself around Godly men and flirt with the one that catches your eye.

Men, it's okay to take off the mask to reveal your true desire for a wife and impatience with finding her. Seize the moment and date the beautiful woman that God places in your path all the way to the altar. Marriage truly is one of the most beautiful experiences on this earth and I want each of you to experience and enjoy it for yourselves.

Your path may take longer or much shorter than you imagine because the Lord works in mysterious ways. In this case, God instructed Doc to write a book about relationships and finding the *one* before he actually found her for himself. His faith landed him on the radio where he was able to be transparent and demonstrate his *faith with works*. Little did he know that God was simultaneously answering his prayers by affording him access to his future wife over the airwaves.

As it turns out, God was positioning Summer for marriage two long years ago by releasing Anthony and Meagan's negative energy from her life and making her dependent upon Him to find her husband. In the end, all she had to do was read a book and allow the author who wrote it in hopes of meeting her to gain access to her.

God was working their marriage long before they ever met. Both kept the faith despite obvious clues as to when and where their soul mate would appear. While Doc and Summer were praying in their individual homes, God was aligning their paths to cross at exactly the right time.

I want each of you to have this type of testimony. I want you to keep the faith and to believe in your ability to find the lasting love that you desire and deserve. You are the solution to the man of your dreams problem. He cannot find you and is waiting on your assistance. Please ease his pain and provide this lucky man with the opportunity to meet the *one* woman he's been so desperately seeking.

Ladies the time has arrived for you to lead him to chase you. Be the total package that he desires and then get your ring finger ready because inside of that Tiffany & Co. blue box is your diamond ring. Cue the orchestra and pop the champagne!

APPLICATION SECTION

Women who make the first move with subtle, yet classy, flirting get more attention and subsequent dates, thereby increasing their chances of finding an ideal mate. These women have a strategy and frequently are surrounded by men who wish to court them. What do they do that affords them so much more attention that the average woman? The answer will not surprise you because it is so incredibly simple that every woman can do it.

First, these women do not misinterpret *He who findeth a wife, findeth a good thing* to mean sit around and wait on a man. Instead, they focus on the fact that men are actively looking for a good thing and make it easy for him to find her. They are able to shake off discouragement, impatience and fear and move with the confidence of knowing that they are the solution so many men are seeking. This confidence allows them to take a bold approach and enter the lion's den. Are you ready?

Good. Here's what I want you to do. Do some homework and strategically position yourself at places where your caliber of man is likely to frequent. Be sure to select events where the male to female ratio is almost certain to be in your favor (i.e., Chamber of Commerce meetings, business networking events, fraternity and male conferences, sports bars, political fundraisers, sporting events, men's ministry, etc.). Find a reason to be there that makes you feel comfortable and initiate operation F.L.I.R.T.

Why can't a woman network and exchange business cards? You have business about yourself too. What's wrong with volunteering at fraternity conference or two? Why can't you watch the game, get more informed about who's running for office in your community or become more active in the male mentoring campaign at the church?

Remember, men are looking for you and if you just so happen to help 1,000 strapping, single and eligible men register for their annual conference then so be it. Trust me, the man who catches your eye will not think twice about your ulterior motives because he'll be too busy thanking his lucky stars. What are the odds of him meeting the woman of his dreams, in of all places; a men's conference. Isn't God good!

Now that you have solved the problem of access by consistently positioning yourself among a large number of eligible men, the next step requires confidence and tact. You must initiate conversation to get him to personally notice you. Believe it or not, you can be assertive and entice the appropriate chase if you play your cards right. Here are a few creative ways to do just that:

1) Smile and speak

Smile and speak upon first eye contact with no hesitation by simply greeting him. This way, you are certain to come off as cordial versus pressed. Then use your eyes to flirt as you walk quickly past him. If he is interested, he will chase you to find out your name. Didn't your grandmother teach you that trick? All men have a difficult time allowing an attractive, confident woman who speaks to him first walk by without at least making her acquaintance.

2) Give him a compliment

Give him a compliment ("nice shoes") and don't say another word. Now allow him to pick up the conversation and meet the gorgeous, intelligent and confident woman behind such kind words. Maintain your composure and allow him the anxiety of wondering if you are just being cordial or actually like him. His pride will kick in and he'll then try to impress you and the chase will begin.

3) Send him a drink (non-alcoholic)

If you are really feeling confident you can send him a non-alcoholic drink. This is a very bold move but it works! I speak from experience. Here's what is likely to happen. By sending him a drink, he feels compelled to walk over and personally thank you. When he approaches, it's time to play it cool. He is expecting you to jock him so, instead, say absolutely nothing except, "You're welcome." Now he's perplexed because his initial assumption about you being desperate is challenged. If he asks why you sent him a drink respond with something witty like, *"You looked thirsty and in need of some great conversation"* and smile. Now, he thinks that you are amazingly confident, clever and funny and wants to learn more about you. The rest is up to you. Besides, he won't let you pay for the pineapple juice anyway.

4) Use Social Media

A less obvious yet equally effective approach is to use social media cleverly. Consider sending a man you find attractive a Facebook request. However, make sure that your profile is reflective of a woman of class, fun and confidence. By all means, please remove all "sexy" pictures that position you as a sex kitten. Leave something to his imagination so that he is compelled to chase. Now just wait for him to message you and allow him to do the major lifting from there.

Another method is to leave a positive comment on his profile page based on one of his status updates. Trust me, men always notice unknown women who comment on their page. He will likely follow you via social media and inbox you to initiate the flirting.

5) Make Eye Contact

The final strategy is probably the easiest, most effective and natural way to attract more attention: Make eye contact and smile. Look him directly in the eye and invite him to meet you and then look away. Do not look at him again until he approaches. The more confident you feel, the more he will be drawn in to find out more about the woman behind the smile.

Interestingly, this is one of men's biggest complaints. "Women just look so mean and don't smile anymore...it's like they don't want a man to approach them," is a frequent refrain from men worldwide. So use your smile as invitation to meet a phenomenal woman. See, you just did him a favor. I'm proud of you.

I really could go on and on with different strategies but I think you get the point. The key is to be confident that you are a gift for the man who interests you. Be convinced that once he meets you, he would be a fool to pass up on an asset like you. A quick caveat, however, please screen wisely and observe before you initiate contact. Not every man deserves to meet you or will respond like a gentleman so be careful.

I would imagine that you may have strong feelings about these strategies but remember that I am a man so they may very well work. Honestly, all five of these techniques have lured me before. However, don't rely solely on me, ask your father, brothers and male friends and get their perspectives too. Their answers might just surprise you and influence the way you date from now on. Men love confident women so why not take control and introduce them to one tonight?

The simple and undeniable truth is that men need you in order to be the best man that they can possibly be. After all, you are our rib. What man wants to wander the Earth missing a rib for his entire life? I have been quoted as saying, "If we are Clark Kent before we meet the one then we transform into Superman as a result of marrying the one." What man doesn't aspire to be Superman? I'm serious. Have you noticed that the large majority of highly successful, healthy and truly happy men are married who thank their wives every opportunity they get? That's certainly not by chance.

Many question why this image of men is not widely portrayed in the media? It's because the men who can best testify are probably sitting at home with some peach cobbler in their mouths, getting their heads rubbed and enjoying a movie with their wonderful wives.

Seriously, I want you to look around and begin to see reality versus media headlines. There are men all around you who wish to settle down and marry just like you do. However, there is one major difference that you must be aware of and respect no matter how painful: Men do not believe in settling!

Men prefer to remain single for life versus marry a woman who does not add up to their unique ideal of the one. Despite missing a rib, they are self-sufficient enough to make due and hold out for the perfect fit. Being cute, intelligent and sexy are not enough; you must prove to be a lifelong asset.

You must desire to be the source (outside of God) where he powers up, feels loved and draws strength. Champion his Superman dreams until they are realized, never forgetting than an asset is always treated as such in return. Remember that self-value translate into added value for him by marrying you. He'll make that fact official with a diamond ring too. Why? You shouldn't have to ask silly. Everyone knows that diamonds last forever and "ring formula women" date for keeps!

Get ready for your final set of homework. Are you up for the challenge? Explain how you can be an asset to a man's life in each area. If you haven't found your Mr. Right yet, then you'll have to go on faith, like Summer did. Faith is defined as both the substance of things hoped for and the evidence of things not seen (Hebrews 11:1). So, chose to believe that your man is on his way. God might work quickly too so you better get busy.

List the ways in which you can be an asset to the man of your dreams in each area of his life.

Financially

help him put money away

to invest.

Psychologically

I can make him feel like

a king by listening to him

and help him to feel good

about himself.

Physically

I could work out w/him and support his extra carricular activities

Health

I could cook heatthy meals, make sure he take his medicine if needed, and shop for heatthier options.

Parenting

I would make sure to teach and be a role model and help raise the kids.

Friend

I could listen to him, support his career and enjoy it with him, be fun, and appreciate him.

CONCLUSION

PUTTING IT ALTOGETHER: WORKING YOUR RING FORMULA

"Simply reading this book is not enough. You must put the Ring Formula to work for you."

Congratulations on completing this leg of your journey! You have all the tools and information you need to be the only *one* your current or future husband ever needs. It is up to you to master these techniques and claim the man of your dreams. You understand the needs of men and have a clear insight on how to meet those needs better than any other woman. By employing what you have learned, you'll be successfully dating and married in no time.

I must caution you, however, that a great man will not fall out of the sky simply because you purchased and read this book. Put into action what you have learned immediately to empower yourself and allow the law of attraction to work for you. As a woman with a great ring formula, you now know how to nourish a man's soul, you should be confident in your inner and outer beauty, maintain a glamorous attitude and self-image, understand how to lead from the side, focus on friendship over lust, refuse to settle for less than monogamy, F.L.I.R.T like a wife, and successfully deal with a man's family.

Prepare yourself, and your MR. RIGHT will find you. Contrary to popular belief, there are plenty of eligible MR. RIGHTS who are ready to settle down and marry. Forget the statistics because remember, you only need *one*. Get used to your newly found power and don't hold anything back. As you put your ring formula to work, you are bound to encounter men who still don't wish to settle down. Don't get discouraged or second-guess yourself. Sometimes, you must pan through the dirt to get to the true gold. Relax and work your ring formula just the same because you will not be on the market long!

Your new theme song is Beyoncé's *Irreplaceable*, so act like it. Consider all the women presented in this book. They are real (names and some details changed to protect the innocent), as are their outcomes. Just like you, they were on a quest for love. Let us review what you should have learned from each situation.

You learned that you could be happier being Julia than Angela because you know the key to a man's heart is through nourishing both his stomach and his soul.

It is better to be Alena than Sabrina because you want to project security to your man. After all, the relationship cannot be secure if you are not yet secure with yourself first. Take time to deal with insecurities when you are single, so they will not become gorillas that work to destroy the good relationship that is on the horizon.

Develop the Karen inside of you because there is no one more powerful than a strong and supremely confident sister with a warm and sincere spirit.

Follow Latoya's example and learn to accept that leading from the side is better positioning than leading alone. Most importantly, remember that a man is fiercely loyal to a woman who demonstrates that she believes in him for better or for worse.

If you need it, seek relationship coaching like Jasmine. Jump off that soul train of dead-end relationships and avoid relying on sex appeal to attract men. Coaching and therapy are necessities, not luxuries, especially when they work to blossom the beautiful woman whom God intended for you to be.

Pull an Erika and bypass all brothers who want to box you into settling for anything less than you deserve. You can do better by yourself by not allowing him to play on your desire for intimacy. Remember, when you exhibit the strength of Erika, the real men will come knocking in no time.

Dust off those psychology books as you conjure up images of Keisha. Make it clear who is running the show now. Befriend his mom because she's your best ally, and behave as the first and leading lady regardless of how many ex's or babies' mamas surface.

Karen embodies the qualities and confidence that every woman should possess. Use your inner and outer beauty, charm and instincts to attract MR. RIGHT. Expect that things will go well and dare to share your magnificence with the world. You were born with purpose; beauty and class so flaunt it and be your own celebrity. Don't allow past hurts to dictate your future. Strive for what you know you deserve, taking no prisoners along the way.

Stop wasting precious time and take charge of your life like Summer did. Rely on your faith in God and take action. Don't wait around for a man to find you. Be phenomenal every single day, position yourself around men and allow the lucky one to make your acquaintance. Be bold, confident and assured of your ability to make a man truly happy. Keep your mind, body, and spirit in tip-top shape and walk like the solution to his problem and he will find you!

No man wants a half-stepper, so confidently parade your full stride. Leave your man no choice but to love you because you give the very same love that you deserve. Get rid of the negative relationships in your life that will pull even the strongest women down. Step out of uncomfortable constraints and give the world all the love your heart can generate. Remember, cream always rises to the top, so develop the richness of spirit from within. Be ready to experience the positive boomerang effect that bountiful love will produce and flirt like a woman who is about to get a ring on her finger.

I am aware that many of the women who read this book believe they already know everything there is to know. No one can ever know everything, so use these lessons as a refresher course. For the novice who readily admits her need for instruction, be patient and allow God to guide your steps toward marriage.

For the seasoned pros who are ready and willing, be patient yet assertive like Summer was and allow God to do the rest. If you know one of your girlfriends, colleagues, family members or sorority sisters who may need this book, purchase a copy, read it together but do your own separate exercises.

Visit www.drtartt.com and www.ringformula.com for additional resources, to learn about online and live seminars, speaking events and book signings in your city near you. Also, don't feel shy about contacting a relationship coach to provide individual assistance in dating towards marriage. I look forward to receiving all your testimonies detailing the wonderful success you have by working your ring formulas to perfection.

I wish you the best on your journey and pray that this book will remain a valuable part of your library. You have taken an important step in your quest to develop your understanding of dating towards marriage and obtaining your very own MR. RIGHT. May you find the love that you deserve. After all, you are the only *one* he'll ever need.

God Bless,

Alduan Tartt, Ph.D.

Answers to the Questions You Always Wanted to Ask ...

Many readers feel compelled to contact me after reading this book to ask a wide variety of questions. Unfortunately, I cannot answer all of them due to the volume and complexity but I do answer many of them. Being a continuous servant, I decided to answer as many as I could in this section in hopes that they provide the needed insight, advice and encouragement to improve your personal relationships.

It is my hope that my transparency as a man will translate to a better understanding, appreciation and love for men in general. Please understand that these answers do not apply to all men but do represent a large percentage who are actively waiting to meet, date and marry a woman like you.

WHY AREN'T YOU MARRIED?

Dr. Tartt: Actually, I'm working on it as we speak-relative to the real time release of this edition. Didn't you read the last chapter? It might have been about me (smile). Seriously, I will allow God to dictate the right time which I hope is soon and just concentrate on getting myself prepared to be the best husband I know how to be each day.

ARE YOU MR. RIGHT?

Dr. Tartt: Absolutely! However, I by no means feel more equipped than the next man to experience lasting love. I realize that only prayer and hard work will see me through. I intend to learn from my past mistakes and rely on God, friends and family for support so that I, too, will have a marriage that lasts forever. I believe that there are many Mr. and Mrs. Rights out there and it is absolutely my intent to get them to date and marry one other.

WHY DID YOU WRITE THIS TYPE OF BOOK?

Dr. Tartt: I wrote this book because God created me to be a helper and I simply could not resist the urge to give dating advice- even to women I was currently dating. I figured, "Wow, if only she knew how much power she's not using but it's too late now." I was surprised how many beautiful, talented and charismatic women needed a reminder about how powerful they were. I figured that I could also help myself get married by showing love first and praying that it would be returned.

Another reason I wrote the book was that I kept seeing reports on the internet and television about how many single women were nervous and frustrated about the possibility of never finding a husband. So I decided to write an inspirational dating guide that helped women find their power and self-confidence while dating and The Ring Formula was birthed.

In summary, I simply wanted to help the only way I knew how. The amazing thing about God is that he has a way of enhancing your vision in a manner far greater than you can ever imagine. I believe he does that so that we are prepared to give him credit versus worship ourselves. As a result, not only are people reading this book, getting engaged/married but also creating new ways for single people to connect and meet. Isn't God good?

WHY WOULD A MAN MARRY WHEN HE HAS SO MANY AVAILABLE OPTIONS TO HIM?

Dr. Tartt: The obvious answer is that men do not perceive themselves to have a lot of options, unless you are talking about sexual encounters, girlfriends or friends with benefits. Most men do not report that they have a plethora of options when it comes to finding a wife. In fact, the majority of men are single because they have yet to find the one woman who is worthy of being called his wife. Men do have a lot of eye candy to choose from these days but too much candy is bad for you and leaves you exhausted, weak and malnourished. After a man is done playing he will undoubtedly begin a quest to find a wife of substance who will nourish his mind, body and soul for a lifetime.

Another reason that men chose to settle down with one woman is the simple fact that he is in love with her and only her. Men are possessive and don't want another man taking what belongs to them. Men understand that only a wedding ring makes the woman he loves his officially and permanently. Additionally, most men have dated numerous women before they decide to marry and are keenly aware of how difficult it is to find the *one*. Once you find her there really is no need to date any further.

WHY DO MEN SEEM TO BECOME DISTANT WHEN THE RELATIONSHIP APPEARS CERTAIN TO HEAD TOWARDS MARRIAGE?

Dr. Tartt: This is a common complaint that I hear from women. The answer is simple. Men are very practical and realize that marriage takes commitment, certainty and money. Thus, they conduct a self-evaluation to determine whether they are ready to be in a committed relationship. Has he been with all the women he cares to be with sexually? Is he sure that he's in love with her and not just sex? Can he really look himself in the mirror and honestly say that he will be faithful for better or for worse? These are some of the basic questions most men ask themselves before actually proposing.

Additionally, men don't want to wonder if they could have found a better wife. Men don't want to settle and have the roaming eye their entire life. Additionally, he doesn't want the drama associated with falling out of love with his wife, losing sexual desire for her and living a lie by pretending to love her when he really doesn't. So, a lot of men extend the courtship process to buy more time to mature, assess and decide whether to marry now or later.

Men also become distant and begin to work longer hours because they realize that marriage takes money. They immediately start calculating how many funds are needed to purchase a wedding ring, finance the wedding, honeymoon and provide a financial security blanket for his wife to be. Additionally, men begin to control their spending and improve their credit scores to ready themselves to be head of household. Additionally, most men still follow the tradition of asking their girlfriend's father for his blessing to marry his daughter. Thus, men prepare themselves for the father to inquire about his finances and ability to take proper care of his daughter. No man wants to disappoint, and, thus saves up enough to confidently assure her father that his daughter is in good hands.

A final explanation for men delaying marriage is that some men are just really scared that the woman will change after he marries her. He wonders if she really loves him or just wanted to have wedding. Additionally, he fears losing his autonomy and his wife changing for the worse (stops cooking, gains weight, disrespectful) because she has what she wants already (the ring) and, therefore, no longer feels the need to work to earn his affection, loyalty and love.

I'M ALREADY MARRIED BUT I'M AFRAID MY HUSBAND MAY GROW TIRED OF ME. HOW CAN I KEEP HIM HAPPY?

Dr. Tartt: Research by Dr. Patricia Love indicates that married men can best be satisfied by implementing the S.T.A.R acronym.

S- Sex
T- Touch
A- Appreciation
R- Respect His Routine

Men do love sex and need to have a lot of it to remain happy. It is not uncommon for men to desire to have sex three to four times a week to feel totally satisfied. Research also shows that men require two to three times the amount of physical touch in order to feel loved. Think back to high school in the hallways where the boys didn't really want to talk with you or carry your books. They really just wanted a hug (touch) and did the necessary things to get one. Not much changes when men mature because they still prefer touch over words. Men like for their back, biceps, neck, feet and head to be stroked and caressed lovingly. It should be noted that touching is the primary way boys bond with their mom. It is not uncommon to see boys cling to their mother longer than girls do.

Research also indicates that most married men feel underappreciated. This is surprising to most wives because men typically do not communicate that need. The truth is that men really expect you to naturally appreciate the things that they do for you (even if it is as simple as moving the couch or washing your car). Appreciation makes men feel adequate, loved and assured that you are still satisfied and happy with them.

Finally, you must respect your man's routine. Men are typically consistent and very predictable beings. They need their routines to feel a sense of normalcy and balance in their lives. They need to watch football, read the paper, wash the car, cut the lawn, play golf, etc. to maintain their autonomy and peace of mind. Don't try to change their routines because you have other needs. Respect their routines and shoot for either adjusting them or acquiring routines of your own that either match or coincide with his. For instance, if he wants to watch football on Sunday afternoon, you can either watch it with him or arrange a shopping excursion with your girlfriends. That way you are both entertained and respectful of each other's routines.

WELL THEN HOW SHOULD MY HUSBAND TREAT ME TO KEEP ME HAPPY?

Dr. Tartt: Research by Dr. Pat Love also gives an acronym for keeping women happy in a marriage. According to her research women are happiest with their men R.O.C.K

R-Routine
O-Open Your Heart & Mind
C-Contact
K-Keep It Positive

Women love it when men are consistent by keeping their routine of calling, texting or asking for quality time. Put simply, don't start out calling every night and then call every other day, then a week and then occasionally. That is enough to drive women crazy and makes them feel unloved and disconnected. Men, keep your routine of calling to check on her, informing her that you will be late and taking her to the Saturday afternoon movies and your woman will thank you.

While men need to connect to talk, women need to talk to connect. Thus, husbands must use words to articulate your affection and love for your wife. It is not enough that she cognitively knows that you love her; she wants and needs to hear you say that to be happy. Also, just like men, women need contact to feel loved. Holding your wife's hand, playing with her hair, giving her a foot massage and/or letting her snuggle under you all communicate love.

Finally, wives rely on their husbands to keep it positive. Men are typically calmer than women are and relied upon to calm women down and create an air of happiness. Men have the uncanny power of making problems seems manageable and thereby relaxing their wives with a positive and kind attitude. This is especially essential during times of conflict. Husbands who are able to remain calm, kind and positive while their wife is emotional are held in high regard. Women expect men to be able to emotionally handle their storm versus argue back and forth. In a strange way, a husband's calmness is not seen as a weakness but as the anchor that keeps her calm and respectful.

WHY DO MEN CHEAT?

Dr. Tartt: Men cheat for a variety of reasons: Lack of trust, desire to have their cake and eat it too, family history of infidelity, greed, etc. However, I feel the main factor is a breakdown in their primary relationship. Men are simple creatures with very fragile egos that need stroking constantly. Sexual attention from their spouse usually reaffirms their position within the household. Frequent arguing and a breakdown of friendship at home can often damage a man's ego. Men with wounded egos can be extremely needy and are very ripe for the plucking by a woman who is willing to stroke that ego with no strings attached.

Please don't mistake this explanation as condoning the behavior. Cheating always hurts all parties involved (wife, girlfriend, children, extended family, the third party, self) so it is best to work things out directly. My advice is to communicate your feelings to your partner first and allow prayer and more quality time to repair the hole in the relationship at home. Additionally, some men just struggle with being the man God created them to be. My advice would be to become his friend first and prolong the courtship for as long as needed to determine whether or not he can handle commitment.

WHY DON'T MEN CHEAT?

Dr. Tartt: I love it when women ask this question because it demonstrates a rarely discussed truth about men and fidelity: Most men do not cheat on their wives. Most men learn from their past transgressions and try not to repeat them. Some men have never cheated while others learn to avoid the circumstances that led to the negative behavior to empower themselves for the future. The ability to remain faithful is based on self-discipline, communicating needs within your current relationship, knowing one's vulnerabilities and thinking with the end in mind at all times.

For instance, most men know themselves pretty well by the time they get married. They know whether or not they can handle the temptation of visiting an adult club, traveling alone, one on one meetings with a female colleague or not. Most men avoid situations that leave them vulnerable because of past failures. They think with the end in mind and are able to focus not only on the temptation before them but the aftermath.

Regardless of how fine, pretty or provocative a woman can be, it simply isn't worth it all things considered. How do you explain to your wife, daughter, parents, parents-in-law, and friends that you hurt your wife's feelings by cheating with another woman simply because she was attractive? That sounds immature, juvenile and dumb once the temptation has been satisfied.

The two primary reasons listed for why men do cheat are need for variety and feeling under-appreciated at home. Surprisingly, all men feel this way at some point or another within a committed relationship. Men who are able to avoid cheating are successful at communicating their needs to reach a solution. The couple may decide to be more adventurous, spontaneous, or find ways to better appreciate one another.

The final reason for not cheating on your wife is simple. Men fear the drama and fallout from divorce. They also don't want to lose the status as "a great man" or disappoint their wives, children and extended family. Studies show, beyond a shadow of doubt, that married men earn more, live longer and are more social and altruistic members of society than their single counterparts. Thus, married men know the benefit of remaining faithful to their wives firsthand. Happy wife equals a happy life!

WHY ARE SOME MEN COMMITMENT PHOBIC?

Dr. Tartt: There are three things that the majority of good men try to avoid at all cost: 1) Being hurt 2) Hurting a woman and 3) Unnecessary drama.

There is nothing worse than making a woman you care about cry and then having to deal with the intensity of those emotions. It's enough to make men want to cry because we feel like big disappointments, jerks and idiots. So, men compensate by creating emotional distance by avoiding a formal commitment from the start. The thought is, "If I avoid commitment then I can never let her down."

Men also cheat to protect themselves. The flawed and very basic thought is, "If I keep my options open I can also buffer myself from being deeply hurt." The other woman thereby provides a cushion to brace any fall when his feelings are predictably (according to him) hurt by you. It's good old-fashioned self-preservation and usually results from being hurt too many times in the past.

Ultimately, the man in this situation does not trust women and thereby expects to be hurt. So, he does it first to protect himself despite the drama it causes. For these men, control over not being hurt is more important than trusting your partner. After all, trust is what left him broken-hearted, weak and helplessly out of control before.

Quick Note: The ultimate counter-attack for this form of self-protection is to leave the relationship if you are desirous of a long-term commitment. Why? Because when you leave you evoke an even greater fear within a man: The fear of letting "the ONE" walk in and out of his life forever. At this point, he is most likely to enter counseling or change because he wants and needs you in his life.

An additional reason for cheating is a simple one: Some men are not ready for commitment. I know this drives you mad but the reality is that you have to wait on men to be ready to marry. Here's a fact, men decide to marry and *then* search for their wife. Usually men have a list of things they want to do before settling down. This list could include sex with a variety of women, making a certain amount financially, improving himself, a predetermined age, or job stability.

One more reason that men fear commitment is they have a fear of being trapped. Commitment means forever, or at least a really long time, and men fear not being able to live up to that requirement. Additionally, many men fear that their significant other will relax once he is officially *hers* and put on weight, stop respecting him or change in a way that makes him wish for someone different. Men fear being helpless by being in a committed relationship with a woman they no longer like, love or are attracted to sexually.

WHY DO MEN TEND TO ACT RIGHT ONLY AFTER THE RELATIONSHIP IS OVER?

Dr. Tartt: The answer is simple...men like and desire to chase. When you leave a man alone and stop calling him, he has time to actually miss you. Inevitably, he begins to experience a significant decline in personal power over you. He's shocked, "She's not even thinking about me," is usually the sentiment. Hence, when you routinely begin to ignore his calls and demonstrate emotional distance from him, you evoke his drive to reacquire you.

The key is to "never let a man see you sweat" and avoid the temptation of worshipping or jocking him at all cost. Date him as strongly as he dates you and expect that he will reciprocate. The most important thing to remember is that there is power in maintaining an appropriate level of emotional distance from him. In essence, a man cannot be your "everything". You must have a life outside of the man for him to fully appreciate you. When you have your own life it makes a man attracted to your self-confidence.

Strangely, the fact that you don't need him excites him greatly. He views you as a worthy challenge and desires to prove why you need him in your life. Make sure that you milk this power for all it's worth because you will never have more power than in the initial pursuit phase of the relationship. You will be well on your way to long-term commitment and marriage if you are crafty enough to make him constantly pursue you while frequently giving him feedback that his efforts are being noticed.

Be tough and make him put in WORK. Men love a challenge and reward you with a diamond ring for requiring them to improve enough to *deserve* (point of emphasis) a catch like you. You can't be a catch without being on the move first. When you enjoy your life, have ambitions, goals and dreams outside of a man, it evokes a chase mentality because you are progressive. Remember, men don't like easy chases and if you are always in his face, what is there to really chase? What dog chases a cat that doesn't run? Where's the fun, excitement and reward in that?

The best way to illustrate this point is to imagine yourself running through a forest while the man of your dreams chases you. You run fast enough to make him nervous about whether he is good enough to catch you. He responds by lightening his load (other women and distractions-work, pursuit of money, fear of commitment, clubbing) so that he can run faster. While you are running, you are focused on the prize (the altar) and you slow up just enough to let him get closer. Occasionally, you look back so that he knows his efforts are not being ignored. You must give him feedback because, otherwise, he'll interpret you as being disinterested and run after someone who verbally and physically responds to his hard work.

WHY DO SOME MEN LIE?

Dr. Tartt: Usually, because they don't like to hurt women's feelings and assume that lying is a better option than telling the truth. Men assume that they are doing you a favor by not revealing the ugly details.

Another reason some men lie is an unhealthy distrust for women due to past history. They feel "I better lie to her because she's lying or will ultimately lie to me." This allows a man to never trust you, and thus, never be caught off-guard by a woman who lies to him and deeply bruises his ego like his ex-girlfriend/wife, mommy or Stacey did back in third grade. Seriously, a man's early childhood experience with love deeply impacts the way he dates well into adulthood.

WHY DO MEN DATE MULTIPLE WOMEN?

Dr. Tartt: Here's the deal. Men usually date multiple women because they are not quite ready to settle down, enjoy the variety and freedom and/or have not found the one woman who comprises that "total package" of everything they are looking for. So, they date multiple women to create a way of meeting all of their needs. The best way to understand it is to imagine a man combining all of his Transformers (a childhood toy) into a mega-Transformer that is the ultimate prize.

It just dawned on me that there is another reason that men date multiple women. By dating multiple women, men can maintain power and control over their emotions and avoid being too caught up too soon. Let me explain. It's not uncommon for a man to find himself seeking multiple dates when he begins to focus on one, very special woman too much. Why? Because he sees a real future with her and doesn't want to date her like he is pressed. He understands that women desire confident men and dating multiple women keeps him from being too pressed too soon. Once he feels that the attraction and level of commitment is equal then he begins to let the other women go.

HOW DO MEN DISPLAY SADNESS?

Dr. Tartt: It is certainly very different from how women tend to express sadness. We have a tendency to mask our sadness because it is socially unacceptable to be both masculine and visibly sad. Personally, I can shed a tear but it is rare and with the lights off (smile). Usually, what manifests instead, is aloofness and emotional distance. If we feel that you won't listen or may even disrespect us for appearing *female*, then we'll just opt avoid conflict, protect our ego and keep our thoughts to ourselves. Instead of talking, many men will opt to self-heal and work it out on their own terms.

Unfortunately, this approach often backfires and deepens the sadness because we close the loved ones out who can help us. Inevitably, our lovers feel spurned and feel compelled to leave the relationship due to frustration and being consistently rejected. This is the time where men tend to cope with alcohol, drugs, work, sex, etc. Men need to talk and feel heard as much as women do. It's your job as a woman to give him a safe emotional place to communicate his feelings without being judged. Likewise, he must use this space to convey his feelings and open up to feel better.

WHAT IS THAT "IT" FACTOR?

Dr. Tartt: Without a doubt, the "IT" factor is CONFIDENCE. A woman with supreme confidence has the ability to bring even the coolest, top-prized man to his knees. Why? Because being in a relationship with a confident woman makes the man feel more confident in himself (unless he has insecurities). Additionally, men respect a challenge and a woman with confidence signals that she's worth chasing and working for. In fact, a truly confident woman can make a man go crazy trying to acquire her time, attention and eventual love. So, if you want men to pursue you, first fall in love with yourself and flaunt it.

HOW IMPORTANT IS INTIMACY TO MEN?

Dr. Tartt: Ladies, there is power in your softness. Men will rarely discuss their intimacy needs, but I'll contend that there is nothing more meaningful to a man. There is nothing more loving than the soft caress and touch of a woman. This is one area where men desperately need women because men cannot touch themselves. Well, technically they could but it doesn't translate into feeling loved.

Research indicates that men require two to three times the amount of physical affection than women do to feel loved. Thus, a woman who makes common practice of caressing her man's head, back, feet, arms, etc. loves better than a woman who only uses words and deeds to convey her love.

Sex is very important to men but there is a distinct difference between sex and lovemaking. Lovemaking is what keeps men in committed relationships (and vice versa) because it is significantly more intimate and personal. A woman should know exactly how to caress, kiss, and hold her man to convey her depth of love for him. However, lovemaking should only be engaged in within a committed relationship or marriage (from a biblical perspective).

Sex must mean something to him for your relationship to endure. That means that he must first love and commit to you before sexual activity is to occur. If you are married, then you should strongly consider engaging in physical intimacy at least two to three times per week (per the research) to get your man happy. Why, sexual activity is the number one way men feel adequate, loved and appreciated. You can tell a man how much you love him all day but he would much rather you show him. Hello!

WHAT IS A MAN'S DEFINITION OF CHEATING?

Dr. Tartt: Most men define cheating as having sexual intercourse with another woman. He hates the conflict that reporting sexual intercourse with another woman brings. Hence, he is unlikely to tell you he made an error in judgment by kissing, inappropriate verbal or physical contact (dancing, etc.) with another woman. Why? Because he didn't cheat! It's just that simple.

Let me explain because I can feel you about to take issue with that last statement. Physical intimacy does not mean the same thing to men as it does to women. Men can engage in physical activity with women they don't even like while the majority of women would great difficulty in sleeping with someone they dislike. Thus, men figure, "Why confess to something that had no meaning and risk losing the woman I love deeply?" Then why would men do it if it meant nothing, right? The reasons are usually trivial (bored, she initiated it, alcohol, lost focus, opportunity) and men will confess that the behavior was stupid, regrettable and irresponsible.

Hypocritically, if women engage in the same behavior then men are likely to label it as cheating. Men are territorial by nature and struggle with even the idea of another man romantically thinking about touching what belongs to him. Thus, a man will accuse his woman of cheating if he catches her even entertaining another man's advances or attention. Yes, men are strange fruit and very hypocritical at times but you must learn to understand and accept the differences while refusing to compromise your standards. Just because men are prone to do stupid things from time to time does not excuse them from honoring their commitment to you.

WHAT ARE YOUR TOP TURN ON'S?

Dr. Tartt: I love a woman who is supremely confident and even a little mean initially. I like for her to have the attitude that she can have any man in the world because of how well she treats him. Couple that confidence with a passion for God and desire to make a relationship work and I'm in full pursuit mode.

I also love a woman who takes good care of herself. I like it when a woman takes time to do her hair, nails, take care of her body, has excellent hygiene and smells nice. I am fond of a woman who enjoys cooking, hosting, and hospitality because she derives pleasure from making our future house guests feel happy, nurtured and loved. I also like a woman who is funny, friendly and giving. When she is giving of her time and heart, I can't help but fantasize about how great of a mother she would be.

I also like a woman who is very comfortable with her body. She has morals and insists that I commit and marry her to enjoy her essence. However, throughout the courtship she sends frequent reminders about how much she desires me and what I can look forward to. I like to be teased and told exactly what needs to be done to earn her affection. I like a woman who is confident and classy yet privately uninhibited when in an exclusive relationship with me. I do believe this is every man's fantasy.

WHAT ARE YOUR TOP TURN OFF'S?

Dr. Tartt: Actually, I only have a few. I dislike women who insult, defame and curse me. Those are immediate and definite deal breakers. I dislike women who cannot communicate their feelings. I don't like guessing what's wrong and having to suffer and live in an unhappy household because we cannot engage in healthy dialogue. I don't like women who are pessimistic and quick to give up on a relationship. I'm also not keen on women who act like men by being overly assertive or aggressive with their words (not to be confused with strength which I like). Finally, I don't care too much for women who keep a messy home. It makes me feel like she would not be unable to effectively run a future household of children.

WHAT ROLE DO YOU THINK THE WOMAN SHOULD PLAY IN A RELATIONSHIP?

Dr. Tartt: I firmly believe that women should rule from the side because men need the title as head of the household for their egos. Women who don't take offense with that are smart because they understand that the title does not dictate actual power and recognize the importance of gender roles.

By allowing her man to take the lead, she affirms his position as the head and endears herself to her thankful husband. She follows his lead which evokes the desire to care for, protect and secure her.

A woman who knows how to *play* (emphasis on the word play) her role is rewarded with devotion, loyalty and more power. By experience, she knows that her man will likely ask her to run the household, make certain business decisions and take the lead on the majority of family decisions because she is better equipped. Because she's smart and understands men, she knows that men don't really want to be in control all of the time; they just want you to say that they are.

Even the dumbest man knows that he is no match for a woman. Women are blessed with the God given ability to multi-task and care for the entire family unit as a whole. She can help the kids out with their homework, fix dinner, go over a report from work, nurse the baby and provide her man with a honey-do list a mile long all at the same time. Not too many men can do that. Thus, it behooves us to respect our woman's role as the COO (Chief Operating Officer) of the house and support her authority as well.

Additionally, prior to having children, a woman's role should be to improve her man's life in every area. Her influence on his life should be reflected in his overall health, wealth, spirituality, positively, balance and overall life satisfaction. Likewise, men should make their women feel more secure, connected, appreciated, celebrated, desired, relaxed and cared for.

I believe that men and women were not created equal. Each has skill sets superior to the other that work lock in key to complement one another. What one cannot do, the other usually can which makes them more powerful as a team. My advice is to seek ways to compliment and upgrade your mate versus trying to compete with him or her. After all, relationships are about being a team and there are no MVPs in relationships. You literally win or lose together- who cares who caused it? Fix it together every time and you'll enjoy many years of matrimony.

WHY ARE SOME MEN INTIMIDATED BY WOMEN WHO MAKE MORE MONEY?

Dr. Tartt: Interestingly, there are many men who are not intimidated by a woman who brings home more money. However, I would be a fool to suggest that these men are the norm. This subset of men rationalizes, "The more combined income the better." Personally, I think that this is a very healthy approach but I must concede that a man's ability to be at peace with being the secondary source of income is rooted in his own sense of pride and adequacy about his profession, worth and income.

In essence, he must make *enough* so that he no longer needs his woman to validate his financial worth to the relationship. Additionally, a man must be convinced that his woman does not judge his value based on money and shows that with her daily actions. For example, she allows him to have equal or majority power over financial decisions. She consistently verbally validates his importance to her as a lover, protector, father-figure and a friend. She is quick to balance her self-sufficiency with vulnerability and express her need for her man to secure, protect, cherish and anchor her- just like daddy.

I will concede that women who make more money than the average man do have a much more difficult time when it comes to dating for a variety of reasons. First, men want to be providers. Being able to bring home the proverbial bacon validates him as a man. Unlike women, men based their ego and value to a relationship based on their profession and earning potential. A man's work is a large part of who he is. Thus, when his income is viewed as unneeded, he begins to question his overall worth to the relationship and tends to look elsewhere for a woman who truly needs him.

Privately he thinks, "Why does she need me?" This is a dangerous place for a couple to be because men need to feel needed; much like a plant needs water. Men need frequent affirmation and proof that they fortify their woman and are appreciated for what they bring to the relationship. This is why we love it when our significant others asks us to open jars and doors, wash cars, fix things and protect the house. It gives us a constant reminder that we are important, valued and worthy.

Second, men fear that women will eventually emasculate and disrespect their status as head of household whenever finances become an issue. For instance, if the man believes that the best decision for the family is to save more versus take an expensive vacation, he can foresee his wife saying, "I'm having a hard time with you telling me how to spend *my* money. We can afford this. It's mostly my money anyway." This likely will result in the man feeling inadequate and he will likely shut down. A man with no house to lead simply does not feel like a man.

A third reason men avoid women who make more money is simple. They do not feel that they warrant the title "head of household." Hence, they avoid even approaching a woman they deem "out of their league". This is so frustrating to women because many women prefer to defer to their man on making financial decisions, despite the income disparity. Many are even willing to combine incomes because they value the spiritual, emotional and sense of connection that a man provides more than money. Usually, with age, women tend to devalue the importance of a man's income because they realize that all the money in the world can't buy the one thing they value most: A great man.

SHOULD WOMEN SUBMIT?

Dr. Tartt: Yes, yes and yes but that submission should be to God not a man. You must trust God to send you the right man so that you can see the God in him and then submit to that. If your man is not sure of who he is and is lost himself, how is he going to lead you? You can still choose to submit to him but you're going to end up crashing into a brick wall. After all, the blind can't lead the blind.

Additionally, smart men learn to view their significant others as co-captains. By submitting to his leadership on a consistent basis you endear yourself to him and he no longer views you as a potential threat to unseat him as captain of the ship. Men may be simple but we are not fools. We realize that the ship sails faster, farther, and smoother with your help. Thus, we are willing to delegate management responsibilities (even of ourselves) to our more talented better half.

Additionally, a woman who cooks, cleans and prepares her man's bath (special occasions) need not even ask him to wash and wax the car, cut the grass, fix the sink, get the oil changed, change a light bulb or take on a second job to make ends meet because that his job. He appreciates your respect and wants to reciprocate by loving, spoiling and protecting you for a lifetime. Interestingly, this is similar to the way a father views his lifelong relationship with his daughter(s).

WHEN IS IT OKAY TO HAVE SEX WITH A MAN?

Dr. Tartt: For the record, I believe that couples should abstain from sex until marriage. While many men struggle with this notion, I do believe that they want to be successful at building a relationship that will last. Here's the dilemma: Most men are assertive, complimentary, flirtatious, confident and display their emotions through physical affection versus words. Hence, it can be difficult for them to feel or show love without being physical.

Many men of faith desire to avoid sin while dating but will inevitably pursue and make sexual moves if really interested in you. However, if you give in too soon, they are likely to experience inner turmoil. What usually incurs is one of those awkward talks were the guy begins to pull away and explains, "It's not you but me". In reality, however, it was you despite him making the first move.

What may have happened is once his sex drive was satisfied, guilt and disappointment occurred about not honoring his faith. Privately, he wishes or even articulates that he needed you to have been strong enough to resist his advances. I know that this sounds very hypocritical and confusing since he initiated the act, but that is how men think at times. In reality, the best move would have been to resist his advances and stand your ground while verbalizing your desire but not at the cost of compromising your morals.

Yes, you will have to endure a mantrum (male tantrum) in the short term but you will take a large step toward building a relationship that has the chance to succeed in the long-term. I'm sure that most men will be quite perturbed by being rejected but the days following are likely to be followed by a new found respect, growing love and intensified courtship. Ironically, he likes you even more because you are making him a better man by challenging him to wait and respect your value. It's like refusing to drop your price because he really wants you. Despite getting upset that his efforts are inadequate he loves the challenge, respects you more and then works his tail off to deserve you.

Please note, however, that men do require a lot of affection (touching my muscles, caressing my hair, etc.) since you have decided not to be sexually active. However, you must have a conversation with him about how much is too much without engaging in the full act of sex. It is very difficult for even the most strong-willed man to resist the temptation of a woman sleeping in his bed so clear boundaries will need to be exercised.

Believe it or not, the power lies with you. Your requirement for how a man is supposed to behave largely dictates how you will be treated. A man who is truly interested in marrying you is unlikely to leave the relationship because you won't give into his advances. Subconsciously, men expect and need you to be different from the other women they have bedded in the past. This makes you worthy of being his wife because you are requiring him to mature, be self-disciplined and a man worthy of being your husband.

In contrast, most men are not actively involved in the church like they should be and may not hold strong religious reasons for abstaining. However, the same rules apply because at the end of the day, men respect women who tell them "No". Be prepared to lose a few men who are only interested in being physical along the way but that's fine. You are not looking for sex; you are looking for a committed relationship and marriage. Ironically, you will find that those same men will come back into your life once they are marriage minded because you were not the problem, their mindset was. Sometimes, men have to experience empty sex to realize that it's not as fulfilling as making love to someone they really care about.

As a quick caveat, it is important that you express sexual energy towards your man to avoid coming across as stiff and boring. You must convince him that you physical love is worth waiting for and he is assured of not being disappointed. The way you look at him, the way you move your hips, and the way you touch him tells him everything that he needs to know. The idea here is to feed a man one chip at a time to keep him hungry for more. If you lose patience or buy into his rationale of "sampling the milk before buying the cow", he is likely to taste and run. Plain and simple, it's manipulation and he knows it. Men seek a total package when it comes to marriage not a sex kitten. If that was the case, every adult entertainer would be married.

You will save yourself a lot of heartache and rejection if you remember that sex only means something special to men who are already in love with you, despite how passionate it may seem. If you are playing for keeps, keep him hungry during the courtship and then feed him and feed him well on your wedding night! Also, don't be surprised if he is now suddenly the one rushing you to the altar because he can't wait any longer to express his love for you. That's what likely worked for your mother, grandmother, etc. and it will work for you as well. Good luck!

WHY DO SOME MEN LIKE YOU BEFORE SEX AND THEN HATE YOU AFTER?

Dr. Tartt: Because they didn't like you as much as they initially thought but didn't have enough time to figure it out. A man's sex drive can confuse him because he's unable to separate his fondness for the woman from how she makes him feel. Often times, it's not until after sex that he experiences clarity as to whether he really likes you or not. More times than not, when sex occurs prior to having a committed relationship, the man's interest declines and he distances himself from you.

As it turned out, his infatuation with you was based on your sexual connection not an emotional one. This can get really confusing for women who date passionate lovers because it feels so intense. He must love you, right? Wrong, he's just a passionate lover who is adept at making love to your body but not the whole package.

If you find a man complementing you on the way you have sex with him versus how much he cares for, needs and wants to spend more time with you then your relationship is likely to fail. After all, he's basically saying that he likes your sex versus you. I realize that this may sting but I would rather you know upfront so that you can avoid mistakes later. The moral here is that you must wait until a man truly cares for you before you even need to think about having sex with him. There is a purpose to abstinence.

HOW SHOULD YOU LOVE A MAN WHEN YOU'RE ANGRY?

Dr. Tartt: I want to share a fantasy I have about dating a woman who is upset with me but still loves me. Here's the scenario: I have been working extra hours at work to achieve a new position within my company. I've promised to spend time with her for months and designated Friday night as *our time*. I indicate that I will be home no later than 8:00 in order to enjoy dinner and a movie. However, while at work, things go haywire and I am not able to leave until 8:30. I make the poor decision not to text but not call. I indicate that my new time of arrival will be 9:00. What should you do?

A) Text me back, "Don't even worry about it ... go back to work"
B) Accept my apology and try and catch a late dinner and a movie.
C) Upon entering your house immediately ask, "Why don't you respect my time and feelings? You are so disrespectful."
D) Allow me to explain first and then tell me your feelings with the corresponding consequence if it happens again and ask me how I plan to make amends?

If you answered (A) - Wrong.
If you answered (B) - Wrong.
If you answered (C) - Wrong.
If you answered (D) - Get your ring finger ready!

Why? Option (A) only conveys that you are angry, and rightly so, but does not do anything to repair our relationship. In essence, you are punishing me by rejecting me. Yes, I am 100% wrong but what good does it do the relationship to tell me not to come home. Ladies, be careful what you ask for because it could lead to a break up.

Option (B) is wrong because it says that you are doormat under these circumstances. Remember, this is becoming a monthly pattern not a random slip. If you opt to say nothing and go on with the date with me as if nothing happened, I may assume that you are okay with it. I'm relieved that you didn't yell at me and behave like I never did anything wrong because it appears that it does not bother you. Over time, I may become too comfortable with your leniency and take your kindness as a weakness.

Why? Because the inner voice inside says, "She's the coolest woman I've ever met...she won't even be upset...I'm going to work a little bit longer". In reality, you are not cool but convey that you are which leads to miscommunication. While I'm thinking that you really don't care what time I get home, you may be thinking that I love work more than I love you. Over time, our relationship is doomed to fail.

If you chose option C then we could never be together (smile). If there is one thing that men have a difficult time tolerating is being yelled at the second they walk in the door. Even though we may be 100% wrong, your approach is almost guaranteed to lead to a fight because you put us on the defensive. Once emotions are high and you begin labeling most men will either isolate themselves or leave the house, thereby making matters worse.

If you chose option D, call me because I love you. You avoid confronting me and allow me to speak first since I am fault. Of course, I will apologize while you listen and gather the facts. You should understand how much my job means to me without settling for second fiddle. Let me know how disappointed you are that I did not manage my time to take care of my first priority: Home. Inform me that you will be going out by yourself or with your friends the following Friday if I continue to place work over you because you don't need to play second to anyone since you are my wife.

Ask me if I still want to catch the movie since it is too late to eat. Enjoy the movie but don't make love to me when we return home. Instead, hand me a list of things I can do to make up from my transgression. Yes, ladies, this is called making a man work his way out of the doghouse. Men are used to this treatment and know to let their actions demonstrate that they are truly sorry. Chances are that you will get more my punishment that you would have gotten originally, so you win in the end. I win too because it makes me respect you and gives me something to do to make you happy again. Next Friday, I'm likely to take the day off in honor of how well you treat me, besides visiting a Bed & Breakfast is on your list and I'm anxious to get out the doghouse immediately if you catch my drift.

WHY DO SOME MEN PREFER TO DATE COUGARS (OLDER WOMEN)?

Dr. Tartt: Cougars (A term for an older woman who dates a younger man) are popular for a few reasons. Quite often, older women tend to have more experience in managing a family and can better understand and meet the needs of men and their children (if from a previous relationship). Additionally, they typically have more experience with satisfying the physical and emotional needs of men. Because they have achieved success in their own career, they are less likely to view men as competition but complements. Thus, they focus on building him up and helping him to realize his full potential. The combination of looking young while dating with wisdom makes them attractive potential mates for younger men.

WHY DO MEN DATE YOUNGER WOMEN?

Dr. Tartt: The answer to this one is pretty easy. Typically men date younger women to feel younger themselves. Additionally, the age difference often translates to an increased level of respect for the man. Younger women also tend to want to have sex more than their older counterparts.

However, it should be noted that a woman's sex drive tends to peak in her 30's versus 20's for men. Remember this is a general rule and does allow for exceptions. It should also be noted that love is love and that people often do not place limits on who they fall in love with. Age truly can be just a number.

WILL MEN MARRY A WOMAN WHO ALREADY HAS CHILDREN?

Dr. Tartt: Absolutely. In fact, some men prefer to date a woman with children, especially if he has child/ren of his own. The fear is not the children but the existing dynamics with the child/ren's father. Is he jealous? Is he open to his ex-dating another man? Will he cause unnecessary drama that could lead to violence? Men don't like mess and prefer that negative emotions be worked out with the children's father prior to entering into a relationship. All men require from one another is mutual respect. If that can be achieved and boundaries are maintained, then the two can coexist peacefully.

Additionally, a major advantage to dating a woman with children is that she is typically more settled, experienced, and better able to run a household because she is already doing it. Hence, they present a ready-made option for men with children or desire children. Men don't have to guess whether they would be a great mother because they see the evidence right before their eyes. So, to all you single mothers out there, keep your confidence up because men do desire what you uniquely bring to the table.

DO MEN PREFER SKINNY OR "THICK" WOMEN?

Dr. Tartt: Men date all types of women. Every man has his particular preference. What men focus on more than a particular body type is how confidently a woman carries herself and her inner beauty. Don't get me wrong, there is nothing more attractive than a woman who takes excellent care of herself. However, men have learned that confidence comes in all shapes and sizes. Hence, if you are confident and know that you are sexy then men will respond positively regardless of your physique. You are what you think about. So, to answer your question, I think most men would chose to date the woman with the most confidence.

DO MEN MIND IF THEIR WOMAN DOES NOT WORK?

Dr. Tartt: I believe that most men just want their woman to be happy. I'm open-minded to whatever makes her happy and benefits us as a family. I would hope that we could sit down as a team and work out any changes to remain on the same page. I also feel that the more children see their parents, the happier they will be. So, if she feels the desire to take a year or more off from work and we can afford to do that, I would be in support of that. I also would consider working fewer hours if money was not an issue to support the family while she worked as well. In my book, the priorities are God, family, and work.

HOW OFTEN DO MEN EXPECT WOMEN TO COOK?

Dr. Tartt: In order to understand why this is so important to me you must appreciate the fact that both my mother and Big Mama are the chefs for not only the family, but the entire community. I equate being a wife with cooking for the family and bringing joy to all who visit our home. I like huge holiday gatherings with friends and family and would love to marry a woman who loved to entertain.

Most men view cooking as a sign of daily love, care and nurturance. Regardless of how much you argue, a woman who still cooks for her man shows that she loves him no matter what. Additionally, it helps him feel secure that their future children will always be well taken care of. In contrast, if you refuse to cook for your man what guarantee does he have that you would make a great mother? What type of mother never cooks for her children?

For the record, I don't like to cook but I can. What makes me want to cook is a woman who enjoys me in the kitchen with her. If an activity brings my partner joy, I'm more likely to participate because I'll probably have fun. I also don't mind washing dishes while she prepares the meal. That's called teamwork and a job my dad still has to this very day. Growing up seeing my dad wash dishes when my mother finished cooking left an indelible imprint on me. Oh and by the way, my momma can throw down so come hard or go home! Okay, I'm joking...kind of. I, like most men, would prefer a great cook but a woman who has a great attitude about learning is just as appealing.

WHY DON'T MEN LIKE TO CUDDLE AFTER SEX?

Dr. Tartt: This is a tricky question that speaks to a much larger question for men who are not married or in a committed relationship. I think the answer for men in relationships is simple. They are tired and want to go to sleep. However, it should be noted that many men don't mind cuddling after sex.

However, for those men who are not in committed relationships, the answer could be a little more complex. Often men are slaves to their sex drive and often don't gain clarity on who they really like until after they climax. Honestly, sometimes it really isn't the man's fault. All men will admit that their feelings and emotions change depending upon their sex drive. There are times during the month where managing their sexual feelings becomes extremely difficult which can lead to irrational and self-destructive decisions.

What I am about to explain will likely shock you but it is my duty to teach you about men so listen up. When a man ejaculates, he experiences a significant decrease in sex drive followed by an immediate return to rational judgment. If he feels guilty, embarrassed, or is not truly attracted to you beyond sex, he is likely to become very distant or even mean. Sometimes, this behavior will occur almost immediately after climax. He cannot believe that you compromised yourself so easily and wants to distance himself from you immediately. He may have enough tact and respect for you to play it off but he will not stick around a second longer than he has to. I don't care if it is 4:30 a.m.; he will get in his car and drive an hour across town to sleep in his own bed to avoid waking up next to a mistake in the morning. Ouch!

This is why it is important to understand men. Sometimes, men must be protected from themselves. You cannot allow men to make decisions based solely on their sex drives because your feelings will be crushed as a result. There is nothing more painful that feeling used by a man who no longer even wants to maintain eye contact with you. He is unlikely to be remorseful either because despite how hypocritical it is, he is disgusted that you actually fell for his sexual advances without requiring him to court and respect you first. Men don't like things to come easy despite asking for it that way. Men respect hard work, especially when it comes to courting.

This is why the Bible speaks out so strongly against premarital sex. Sex, unfortunately, can be used as a harmful weapon outside the confines of marriage. This is why you must have an emotional connection with a man prior to sex so that you are sure his attraction to you is emotional versus purely sexual. To be honest, that's the rationale behind waiting until marriage to become sexually intimate. I'm convinced that we would have far better male-female relationships and more marriages if sex was taken out of the equation for couples who are unmarried. Why? I would imagine that men would marry women faster because they would have fewer options for sowing their wild oats and would base that decision on a genuine love and friendship versus lust which fades as quickly as he climaxes.

HOW SHOULD YOU LET A MAN KNOW THAT HE'S NOT SATISFYING YOU SEXUALLY?

Dr. Tartt: Very carefully. If you tell him inappropriately it will prolong the problem and his ego will be so damaged that he'll avoid sexual contact altogether. However, if you say nothing and the problem continues, he will eventually sense that you are unsatisfied. Strangely enough, he may choose to compensate by stepping outside of the relationship to see if he can please another woman to get his confidence up or even to hurt you before you break up with him. Strange but true.

So, what should you do? Let him know that you care about him and take a scientific approach to the problem. Focus on the problem, not the man. Work together to fix the problem via medicine, change of diet, routine or even sex therapy. Also, the sooner you act the better because a man with no confidence is useless. You will likely lose attraction to him and he'll mope around the house feeling sorry for himself. Be assertive and fix the problem so you can enjoy the mind-blowing love-making that all couples deserve.

WHAT IF I WANT MORE SEX AND I'M NOT GETTING IT?

Dr. Tartt: Then I recommend rekindling what you once had together. Chances are that your sex life was satisfying initially and somewhere along the way you lost your sexual chemistry. This is a common problem for married couples, especially those with children. Often times, couples get so busy managing their career, children, church, etc. that they forget about nurturing their relationship with one another.

So, I recommend starting over and beginning the courtship process again. Schedule time to date one another at least weekly and then arrange other activities around your time with one another. Chances are that your sexual chemistry will resurface when you begin to regularly schedule time with one another. A great movie followed by stimulating dinner conversation could be just the aphrodisiac that you need. If that doesn't work, try male enhancement pills or supplements that boost his libido.

HOW IMPORTANT IS KEEPING A CLEAN HOUSE?

Dr. Tartt: Keeping a clean house is way more important than women realize. Men often gauge a woman's marriage potential based on how she measures up with his mother. Chances are that mom did not keep a dirty house. Surprisingly, men will eliminate you on the first date if your house is unkempt. To men, it makes a statement about you: Messy house = Messy woman.

Surprisingly, men will begin to think into the future (children, family reunions, etc.) before they even meet you in person. If you keep a dirty house then kiss your chances of raising his kids goodbye. I dated a woman whose house was a mess and immediately I decided that I could never talk to her again. She went from a 9 to a 0 within one look at the dirty kitchen floor, clothes on the floor and collection of unwashed plates next to, not in, the kitchen sink. Since I'm a nice guy, I continued with the date anyway but I sure wish I could have disappeared. Yuck!

The interesting thing is that men are often hypocritical and may even have an unclean home themselves. This actually makes sense when you think about it from the eyes of a man. As a boy, his mother either cleaned his room or made him do it himself. However, rarely did he see his mom's room in disarray. Most men expect the woman to at least manage the household responsibilities. If you can't even manage to keep your own home clean how can I see you in mine? For the record, men with dirty houses are less attractive to women but it's not as big of a red flag as a woman who is untidy.

WHY IS IT SO DIFFICULT FOR UNMARRIED COUPLES TO HOLD OUT ON SEX?

Dr. Tartt: This is an excellent question because most Christian women agree with the idea of no sex until marriage. However, many find it very difficult to execute in the current sexual revolution where premarital sex is the norm- even within the church. Here's the dilemma as it was described to me. If you withhold sex from your man he will grow disinterested and either cheat or end the relationship. If you engage in premarital sex then you sin, feel badly, and compromise the structure of friendship that makes relationships last.

Further complicating the matter is the fact that modern forms of dating are not conducive to non-sexual relationships. For instance, many couples are spread out and travel to see one another. In major cities, it's not uncommon for someone to live fifty minutes to an hour away. Thus, if you date on Friday or Saturday night, inevitably one of you will be tempted to spend the night to avoid a long, dark drive home at midnight. Over time, especially if drinking is involved, you are likely to engage in some form of physical affection that can easily lead to premarital sex.

I recommend two things to remedy this problem. One, commit to being abstinent together initially and create ways to share intimacy that don't involve sexual intercourse.

However, be careful, sometimes a little leads to a lot more. I call it the "One Chip Rule". You should only feed your man one chip at a time to keep him hungry and desirous of you. The key is to find the fine line between sharing intimacy and irresistible temptation which differs for each couple.

The second recommendation is to structure your dates accordingly and be self-disciplined. If you know that you have very little self-control on Friday night, especially if drinks are involved, then schedule a date outside of the house where you both meet and leave from the same location. I mean, how much could happen in the parking lot? Don't answer that. In summary, know your limitations and plan accordingly when possible.

DO MEN GET BOTHERED WHEN YOU ASK THEM ABOUT PAST RELATIONSHIPS?

Dr. Tartt: If he does that's a definite red flag for a number of reasons. One, it indicates that there are still unresolved conflict, either within himself or between the two of them. Second, it could be an indication that he's secretive and may have a hard time communicating his feelings in general. Remember that lasting relationships are based on the depth of friendship between two people. Hence, talking about past relationships is absolutely necessary to building a lasting foundation. You can learn an awful lot about a person based on how they responded in previous relationships.

However, I would be remiss not to cover the other end of the spectrum. Sometimes the irritation regarding discussing past relationships is justified. There's a difference between discussing past relationships to get to know someone and comparing your current relationship to those in his past. Past relationships should only be discussed in the context of supporting, learning and understanding one another not as a measuring stick to your own. Additionally, no man, or woman for that matter, wants to hear about the problems you had with an ex while you're on a date. Focus your attention one another, not your ex. Can you say, "Check please!"

ARE MEN OKAY WITH A WOMAN HAVING MALE FRIENDS?

Dr. Tartt: Depends on how secure the man is, how trustworthy you are, and which male friend it is. Personally, I encourage all healthy friendships regardless of gender. However, when it comes to a male best friend who is not homosexual (smile), he must continuously behave in manner that shows respect for my position and be an asset versus a liability. For instance, if he helps our relationship by offering unbiased advice then he's an asset. However, if he consistently puts negative energy and judgment in the air then he is a liability and must go.

Additionally, even the most secure men question the motives of other men, especially single ones. We wonder, "Why doesn't he spend time with his own woman or get a wife himself." Men are hip to the subtle games other men play, especially men who *play* best friend in order to get into a woman's pants. Men are keenly aware that this "best friend" may take advantage of an argument, period of conflict, or time spent traveling to console his woman right into the bed with him. Don't get me wrong, male-female friendships can exist but both parties must meet to establish a mutual understanding.

WHAT'S THE BEST WAY TO STOP ARGUING?

Dr. Tartt: Here's where a psychologist can save you a lot of heartache and pain. The first step is to change your mind set about arguing. How's the saying go? Change a person's mindset before you attempt to change their behavior. Remember that your ability to successfully handle conflict will dictate how long and strong your relationship will be. A fact of life is that all couples argue but only the ones who know how to get through arguments last. So, commit to learning how to argue and handle conflict appropriately.

The ability to handle conflict appropriately is based on preparation, preparation and more preparation. Hence, I recommend discussing how each party desires to be confronted when a problem arises prior to an argument. What a novel idea right? The purpose is to prepare yourselves, like practice, to perform as a loving couple in the heat of battle. For example, if I have already told you that I prefer a soft tone and direct talk versus yelling and screaming then the chances of me responding positively are increased when you take that approach.

My second recommendation is to set a time limit for how long you will argue and stick to it. This involves using a timer (like the ones that come in board games) so that no person is talking longer than their allotted time. Remember, an argument should be a dialogue not a series of monologues, manifestos or uncontrolled rants. Additionally, you should agree to only argue for 15 to 30 minutes (for example) and then move on with the rest of your day. Sounds impractical huh? Not really.

I literally mean move on with your daily activities. There's no greater cure for arguing than allowing time to heal wounded emotions. Again, you should plan how much time each one of you needs to cool down (i.e., 1 hour, 3 hours). It is imperative that you agree on this set time prior to having a conflict so that you are on the same page. There is nothing worse than one partner carrying animosity when the other really wants to make up. In fact, the other partner can grow discouraged, feel rejected and then prolong the conflict to get back at you. If you say one hour then stick to it. Your ability to stick to one hour, for example, is critical to the next step in successfully arguing without breaking up.

Oops, I forgot something. I haven't told you how to argue.

Yes, there is a strategy that leads to successful resolution and often even draws couples closer after a conflict. The purpose of arguing is to ensure that each one of you is *heard*. Again, I repeat, the goal is to simply make sure that each one of you is *heard*. Please rid yourself of the idea of winning an argument. How can a team that argues with itself possibly win? If you hold that opinion you are guaranteed to fail as a couple because every argument will inevitably leave a clear winner and loser which leaves you 50% messed up! Winning is resolving the conflict peacefully where both parties compromise for the sake of the team.

So, throw away the notion of winning unless you want to lose your relationship. Instead, commit to listening to one another at the highest level. Here's how. The first step is making sure that you communicate how you feel versus what you think. Because you are both adults with legitimate life experiences and opinions you will rarely succeed in getting the other person to change his or her mind. By contrast, you can listen to how each other feels and find common ground.

The process involves:

1) Making direct eye contact

2) Stating the other person's name

3) Saying how you feel using an actual feeling word (embarrassed, sad, jealous, unappreciated, neglected, disrespected, etc.).

4) Use a specific example that is current,

5) Tell your partner what you need him/her to do.

6) The listener's job is not to interrupt and to listen attentively because they must repeat almost verbatim what you just said and check for accuracy (this is why the speaker has to be direct, short, and to the point).

7) The roles then reverse until the conflict is resolved or at least both of you feel heard.

I will demonstrate this method shortly but, first, let's review an unhealthy argument style that is characteristic of so many couples:

Gabrielle: "Alduan, I'm getting sick and tired of telling you over and over to stop ignoring and disrespecting me by not introducing me to your friends whenever we go out."

Alduan: [Interrupting] "You don't even like my friends. Why would I introduce *you* to any of *my* friends?"

Gabrielle: "Well, Alduan, maybe I would like your friends if you had better taste or judgment."

Alduan: "See, there you go judging."

Gabrielle: [Interrupting] "I wouldn't have to if you picked better friends."

Alduan: [Interrupting] "Really, is that so? You're so controlling."

Gabrielle: [Interrupting] And you're selfish and childish just like your friends. Why don't you grow up?

Alduan: I am grown. [Exists room]

Gabrielle: See, there you go running again ... just like a kid.

Alduan: Whatever [gets in car and leaves house].

Now, let's try the technique we just learned and see what happens:

Gabrielle: "Alduan, it really makes me *frustrated and unloved* when you don't introduce me to your friends whenever we go out and I need you to introduce me from now on."

Alduan: "Gabrielle, I hear that you feel frustrated and unloved when I don't introduce you to my friends when we go out and you need me to introduce you from now on. Is that right?"

Gabrielle: "Yes."

Alduan: "Well, I feel *uneasy and uncomfortable* introducing you to my friends because you usually judge them and I need you to respect my choice of friends going forward."

Gabrielle: "Alduan, I hear you feel that I make you feel *uneasy and uncomfortable* when I judge your childish friends" (smiling) "...just playing... *your friends* and you need me to respect your choice of friends. Is that right?"

Alduan: "That's right, now who specifically do you want to meet?"

Gabrielle: "Oh no one, baby I love you. Let's go to the movies."

Alduan: "Sure, can I call my friends" (laughing).

Gabrielle: "Keep playing (as she playfully rolls her eyes and the two are off to enjoy an afternoon movie).

Now, you can see how this exchange has the ability to work out if the couple continues to stick to the basic script. We learned that Gabrielle feels unloved and frustrated while Alduan feels uneasy and uncomfortable. Neither party wants to make the other feel that way, but they are actively working through real issues that previously were unstated.

The next step is to begin to repair the relationship to its previous state. In essence, you must make a deposit into the account since the argument undoubtedly created a withdrawal from your relational harmony. So, I recommend that you both plan to do something that you both enjoy. Most couples report that they don't want to talk to one another when at odds which is why I recommend the movies. At the movies, you don't have to talk but you can still enjoy time together. Chances are that you will be holding hands or at least sharing popcorn by the end if you play your cards right. After all, you two are friends right?

Once you've made a deposit into the relationship now it's

time to apologize and make up. You're already set up to succeed. You have each heard how the other person feels, gotten your alone time, enjoyed a movie together and allowed time to be your ally in getting back on the same page.

WHY DO GUYS AUTOMATICALLY SHUT DOWN WHEN WOMEN SAY "WE NEED TO TALK"?

Dr. Tartt: Because of arguments like the one you just heard. Truly, it's a no-win situation if you don't know how to argue towards resolution. Men hate drama, talking for hours about the *same old thing*, and getting nowhere as a result. Besides, men prefer physical touch versus words to bond whereas women usually need words to feel connected and loved. Please understand, your man is not your girlfriend and will not be able to talk to you like one. Take his simple sentences in context with his gender and avoid requiring him to talk to you for hours. He's just not hard-wired that way. I'm not saying that the two of you cannot enjoy long conversations but he is unlikely to talk to you daily like you do with your girlfriends. State your point, stick the script, hold your emotions at bay and allow him to respond like a man and go from there.

SHOULD I CONTINUE TO DATE A MARRIED MAN IF HE TELLS ME HE LOVES ME?

Dr. Tartt: No, but it would be unwise to leave him without first preparing yourself. Why? Because you already know that dating a married man is wrong. You continue to date him because he meets your intimacy needs even if it is on a part-time, secondary basis. At the end of the day, something is better than nothing, right? If you leave him without a back-up plan for meeting your intimacy needs you are very likely to either go back to him or get yourself involved with another married man.

It's important that you understand that once you agree to be a mistress that you lose the power to require monogamy even if he does leave his girlfriend or wife. Despite the problems that may exist in their relationship, men expect you to require full commitment versus settling for second fiddle. What usually occurs is a pattern of cheating for a lifetime. After all, how can you reprimand him for cheating when you participated initially?

The key is to fill your time with friends and family while you break things off so that excessive loneliness does not send you back. Next, you may want to evaluate why you place yourself in situations where marriage is impossible. Avoid settling for what you can get or accepting that all men cheat. Instead, focus on what you want and go for it. Make sure that you feel worthy of a great man and focus all of your energy on truly being happy with your own man.

MY SPOUSE/SIGNIFICANT OTHER AND I ARE FALLING OUT OF LOVE BUT DON'T WANT TO. WHAT CAN WE DO TO SAVE OUR RELATIONSHIP?

Dr. Tartt: I'm sorry to hear that and pray for the best. My advice would be to return to the time in your relationship when things were working well. Evaluate what specifically worked for you as a couple and get back to doing those things. Often times, couples are surprised to learn that they have stopped investing the necessary time to keep their relationship together. In my opinion, married couples should be in engaging in dating and sex at least weekly at a bare minimum.

I do realize that many of you may have children and other obligations but that could be exactly the problem. Those *other obligations* have taken priority over your quality and intimacy with one another. How can you keep a consistent fire going if you don't have a routine for constantly stoking it? You can't. So, call your man in the room right now and ask him to read my reply. Chances are, he'll be more than willing to comply because he wants more love, quality time and peace of mind too. Good luck!

CAN YOU TRULY DIVORCE-PROOF A MARRIAGE?

Dr. Tartt: The research says that you can. Dr. John Gottman is the expert you should consult in this area. If I can summarize an important finding in his work, he states that couples who have the strongest and deepest friendships master the ability to survive arguments based on the strength of their friendships and, thereby are less likely to divorce. In short, the friendship is too strong to allow divorce. It makes sense when you consider your relationship with your best friends. Chances are that you two argue but the idea of ending the friendship permanently is not an option because your bond is too strong. Dr. Gottman has an entire book series on how to rekindle the flame, love-mapping, deepening your friendship, etc. His book is entitled, *Making Marriage Work*. Pick it up today and tell him I sent you.

ANOTHER WOMAN CONFRONTED ME IN FRONT OF MY MAN. I STOOD UP FOR HIM AFTER HE CLAIMED ME AND DENIED HAVING A RELATIONSHIP WITH HER. DID I DO THE RIGHT THING?

Dr. Tartt: I think you did in the short-term because you need to get more information before you listen to an outside person about your relationship, especially another woman. Never let the other woman see you sweat but you do need to find out if there is smoke where there is fire. This, however, should be done in private to avoid giving her the satisfaction of even thinking that she has any power in your relationship whatsoever. Ask your man what is going on and pray that he tells you the truth. Allow his actions to dictate how truthful he is. If he's honest, he will be able to prove it by doing what you ask to alleviate your fears and address your concerns.

I BELIEVE IN NO SEX UNTIL MARRIAGE BUT MY BOYFRIEND AND I ARE GETTING BORED. WHAT SHOULD WE DO?

Dr. Tartt: This is a common problem in an age where it seems like no one is a virgin. Once you've been to the mountain top, you'll likely want to go every time. Anything less, is boring and less stimulating than where you've previously traveled. However, all is not lost because you will have to find ways to keep the sex steamy, fresh and hot when you are married anyway so you might as well start the basics now. Sit down together and explore what things you both enjoy outside of sexual intercourse that still allow both of you to feel excited and loved. You'll be surprised how many things the two of you can come up with but be careful not to go too far because it might make the situation worse.

If you find yourselves being unable to wait under all circumstances despite your beliefs, at least agree to limit the frequency and "fast" in between acts to ensure that your relationship is built on love, connection and friendship and not just sex. However, you do know that you two could just get married and make love daily (laugh).

I'M DATING A GUY WHO IS LEGITIMATELY VERY BUSY. HOW CAN I GET HIM TO SPEND MORE TIME WITH ME?

Dr. Tartt: This is a good one because this is me all day long! First, let me tell you what not to do. Don't demand that he spend more time with you and resist the temptation to question whether he really needs to work that hard. This will only serve to irritate him and he is likely to avoid you altogether for peace of mind, even if you are correct.

Instead, use your skill set to help him accomplish his goals in less time. Be sure to assess his priorities to make sure that a relationship is higher on the totem pole than work, the gym, video games, hanging with the boys before you enter into an exclusive relationship. Men are honest and don't always value relationships over other hobbies and career opportunities that may present themselves. They still value companionship but they are not yet ready to place relationships as a top priority. My advice is to simply befriend him and allow him to pursue you once his priorities change.

If he does value marriage but really cannot figure out how to achieve balance to juggle work, dating and personal care then help him out. Find out what his dreams and ambitions are and find a way to help. Tell him that you admire his work ethic but would like to see him more. Let him know that you are willing to support and help him. The options are limitless- you can bring him food to his job, edit his book, put virus protection on his laptop, spruce up his website, proof his reports, etc. Let him know that he can call on you for support and guidance.

Any woman who is willing the decrease herself to improve a man is like gold to a man because he realizes that she does not have to do this. He will then look to reciprocate because he knows that he works too much and has been waiting years for a woman to understand and support that. Many men show that they love their wives but working more so that his wife can work less. He needs you to balance him out so that he does a great job as a husband, father and community servant.

I'M 30/40 AND NOT MARRIED AND FIND MYSELF GETTING NERVOUS AND DATING LIKE IT. HOW CAN I DATE WITH CONFIDENCE WHEN TIME TRULY IS RUNNING OUT?

Dr. Tartt: I hear you! However, time is running out for men as well. They have time-tables as well regarding the age they desire to have children too but mainly don't want to be the old man in the club who missed out on the prime selection of women. I recommend that you quickly finish your personal goals that make you the best candidate for marriage (fitness, spirituality, healing time, etc. goals) and place yourself in the company of men on a frequent basis.

Remember, men's biggest reason for not being married is the inability to find the one. So, find activities that you enjoy where men will be in attendance and allow them to find you. If the early bird catches worm, why can't an assertive woman catch a man by consistently placing herself around them. If you are the finished product and know how much value you add to men then all you'll need to do is decide which man is right for you. What a great problem to have.

MY BOYFRIEND IS TELLING ME THAT I SHOULD GIVE HIM SEX SO HE WON'T FEEL TEMPTED BY OTHER WOMEN. WHAT SHOULD I DO? I DON'T WANT TO LOSE HIM.

Dr. Tartt: Tell your boyfriend to go jump. Most men won't leave the woman they truly love over lack of sex. If, however, you are rationing out sex for other reasons then he might be telling you the truth. The most dangerous thing that you can do is give in and compromise your morals based on anxiety. He'll use this tactic time and time again or leave you after he gets what he wants in the first place.

So, my advice would be to pass on the manipulation. If he does want just sex that is his prerogative but it doesn't mean you have to stay with him. Give him permission to sow his wild oats elsewhere while you look around for a better fit.

Don't get overly upset if he feels he needs sex. He's only being honest and may not want to hurt you by cheating. Let him go and leave the door open for him to return once he realizes that sex outside of love is highly overrated. Of course, you should date other men because he could very well be replaced with a more mature version of himself.

WHAT QUALITIES MAKES A WOMAN THE ONE?

Dr. Tartt: I am excited about answering this one because I am presently dating an awesome woman who seems to have it all. She possesses a number of qualities that many Mrs. Rights possess but her unique ability to possess so many simultaneously is what makes her the "One". Let me see if I can give you the top five and don't be surprised if you possess them too. That's why I always advocate for women to put themselves in position for men to find you. A man can date his whole life and still not find the "one". Thus, he continues to date until he finds her. Be that "one" and you'll be off the market before you know it.

First, she is a perfect fit or complement for me. She is quiet whereas I tend to be talkative. She is cool whereas I tend to be hype. She is a planner whereas I tend to go with the flow. She is consistent whereas I tend to fluctuate with the tide (typical Piscean man). She is great negotiator whereas I am not. She is patient whereas I tend to want to make everything happen now.

Two, she is incredibly confident. She possesses the quiet type of confidence where she can allow others to be the star until it's her turn. Usually, she has to be asked to speak but when she does she outshines even the brightest star. Then, she goes back into her reserved yet poised demeanor as if she didn't just electrify the room with her words and Godly presence.

Third, she is extremely self-disciplined. If I tell her I need to be more disciplined about working out, eating right, focusing on one project at a time, etc. she creates a plan to make that happen. If we discuss refraining from sexual activity then she does not wilt under pressure. She sets goals every year and accomplishes them. She's a doer and works extremely hard to earn the rewards.

Fourth, she is playful, youthful and incredibly sexy. She loves to have fun, even if it is doing something that takes her out of her comfort zone. She is not one for public displays of affection whereas I will kiss you in front of the pastor but she will go with the flow if she senses my energy is high. She loves life and wants to take amazing trips, experience new things and always has energy to "do one more thing". She works out a lot but is not a fanatic about it. She knows exactly what to wear to put me in the mood and has a dress for every occasion. She is reserved in what she says at times but her attire, body language and smile tell me everything I need to know.

Fifth, she is a woman of God. She has an aura and her smile indicates that she is always one step ahead of me. It is as if she is visualizing what is going to happen next and simply leads me to where God wants me to be. She spends a lot of time thinking about how to assist me in my endeavors and speaks to the God in me. Most important, under pressure, it's obvious that she trusts where God leads her and does not panic. She can weather a storm and make us a stronger couple because of it.

Sixth, she is people person, which is an absolute must to fit with my personality. She can work the room and does not need me to stay by her side to feel comfortable. We can be in the same networking function and speak only a few times or make eye contact to check in and we are both cool. However, what I like the most is that she yearns to help others. She loves hooking up my family members and friends with dates, connecting people with like personalities and interests and getting people together to feel connected.

Seven, she knows how to "handle" me and my family which is amazing. I can be a bit of a workaholic at times because I think so big and I'm naturally driven. Besides, it runs in the family. Instead of complaining, she'll prepare food and bring it to me while I'm working in another room. She smiles and walks in a way that tells me, "Finish your work Babe while you eat this for strength and then take a break and put in some quality time with me."

At family functions, she has fun with my brother and parents. It's not surprising that she'll turn up missing for a few moments while she counsels a relative about a problem. She can sense tension or anxiety in the room and say just the right thing to break the ice or lighten the mood. She likes caring for her grandmother and never complains.

The wonderful thing about this woman is that she possesses all of these qualities without even trying. She just "is". I guess that's the message. Just be yourself and allow God to find the perfect complement for you. There are so many men out there, me included, who have dated for so long in search of the "one". I believe that God has that person preselected for us all and that we meet him/her at the right time. Resist dating just to fill time or forcing a relationship due to anxiety. Your soul mate will present himself at just the right time. So don't give up. He's looking for you while you look for him.

WHAT ADVICE DO YOU HAVE FOR WOMEN WHO HAVE EVERYTHING BUT THE RING BUT THEIR MAN STILL REFUSES TO MARRY?

Dr. Tartt: You mean a wife-y? I was first introduced to term "Wifey" by the R & B group NEXT in 2000. They had a song entitled, *Wifey*, that flew up the charts because it was catchy and talked about love and marriage. However, that was the problem. All it did was *talk* about marriage. In the video, each one of the male singers had a female love interest but not one of them had an engagement ring. I was confused. How can you propose to someone without a ring? Oh, now I get it, will you be my wife-y?

I know you may be thinking, "Well, what's wrong with that?" Well, nothing, unless you ignore the y! By definition, a wife-y is someone who is wife-like but not an actual wife. She provides the man with all the benefits of being married- sex, loyalty, home-cooked meals, raising his kids- but without the actual title and ring afforded to a real wife. That song is a decade old now but it captured the current and growing phenomenon of women settling for being just wifeys. As a man, I couldn't understand why a woman would settle for being an *Almost-Wife* versus a real one and then I met Renee.

Renee sought relationship advice about her long-term boyfriend, Anthony, whom despite multiple affairs she remained faithful to for years. She was growing frustrated with him talking about marriage without actually proposing. He used all the typical tricks. He took her to meet his parents, window shopped for rings and even gave her a key to his apartment with an open door policy which, ironically, is how she caught him cheating each time. Renee was slowly beginning to realize that she would never be a wife, at least not Anthony's, and wanted a professional male's perspective on what she should do.

Renee was beautiful! She had beautiful teeth, full lips, was well cropped and never missed an opportunity to showcase a mean shoe game with matching designer bag, of course. Despite possessing all the fashion sense of Paris runway model, Renee didn't even possess a Wal-Mart education when it came to understanding men.

My advice to her was simple and direct. I advised her to leave Anthony. By her response, you would have thought I accused her of shopping at PayLess. "I know you are not suggesting that I give up everything that I have worked for and endured- all the affairs, the lies, the broken promises- and leave with nothing to show for it, do you?" I calmly asked her, "Renee, what do you really have?" Before she could retort, the weight of the question overwhelmed her and she began to cry. I empathized with her and advised her on regaining the power in her relationship. The advice worked too because within four months, Renee had a ring on her finger. I bet you want to know what I told her, huh?

First, she had to stop allowing fear to drive her relationship. Her fear of losing Anthony, being alone and starting over again was preventing her from gaining what she desired most: A husband. You are what you think about; and if all you think about is not losing then it's psychologically impossible to ever win.

Second, she needed to stop taking Anthony's infidelity issues personally. Anthony's own fears led him to sabotage the relationship every time he felt pressured to marry her. Like most men, Anthony feared being inadequate as a husband. How could he profess to love and cherish Renee for the rest of his life with no track record of being successful in the past? So, he purposely fouled up but not enough to permanently lose Renee, his "wifey".

Third, I empowered her by showing her how to use Anthony's greatest fear against him: the fear of losing her. Men are naturally possessive and their egos cannot handle the idea of losing the woman of their dreams and being forced to helplessly watch from the sideline as she gives *his* love to another man, until death due *them* part. Men dislike feeling ashamed. Thus, avoiding it is a motivator. How could Anthony live with himself knowing that he lost his future wife all because he was *scared*?

Now, there was only one thing left to do. Renee needed to conquer her own insecurities so she could feel confident about leaving. She worked through childhood feelings of paternal abandonment, abusive ex-boyfriends and strengthened her relationship with God, the ultimate Father. She began to see what was so obvious to others yet had been blind too herself- the beautiful child of God who was most deserving of unconditional love and committed relationship. So, with God as her guide, she gathered her belongings and left Anthony in search of a real husband. She explained to Anthony that while she loved him deeply, God's love for her was far greater so she refused to settle for less than equal value. She kissed him softly and walked like a Proverbs 31 woman to her car and sped away.

Poor Anthony couldn't even make it one week before he was harassing her work, texting her daily and stalking her at church. When he did finally track her down, he came prepared and revealed a sparkling two-carat ring and proposed on the spot. She cried, took the ring with no response and made an impromptu visit to my office the first thing Monday morning. She wanted to say thanks, but then threw a curveball that even an ex-baseball catcher turned psychologist didn't predict. She returned the ring and informed Anthony that she would entertain future proposals but not until he entered counseling to deal with his infidelity issues. Besides, she had met someone else and wanted to see if this was the man God promised her. As it turns out, he was a male client whose appointment always preceded hers. His reason for seeing me...couldn't find a wife. Go figure. Isn't God good!

ABOUT THE AUTHOR

D*r. **Alduan Tartt*** is a positive psychologist, professional speaker, parenting, teen and relationship expert as well as a devoted father. He provides positive, empowering and relationship enhancing advice for teen girls and women. He teaches teen girls *how to date boys* to promote women's empowerment while decreasing teenage sexual activity and pregnancy. He is also author of The RING FORMULA: How to Be the Only Woman He Ever Needs, for single women.

He has appeared on ABC Nightline with Steve Harvey and Hill Harper, MTV's Made, CBS Radio, BET Networks TVOne's Black Men Revealed, Fantasia For Real, Gospel Touch and over 30 radio broadcasts. He has served as the resident relationship expert for the Rickey Smiley Morning Show and Darlene McCoy radio shows. He currently is host of his own radio show *On the Couch With Dr. Tartt* in Atlanta, GA.

Dr. Tartt is a frequent contributor to Essence and Black Enterprise magazines and is a monthly columnist for Today's Black Woman, Solo Woman Magazine and Sister 2 Sister magazines. Dr. Tartt recently partnered with author and publisher Curtis Benjamin on *Saving Our Daughters Volume 5 "Who Will Save the Little Girl"* which is supported by Dr. Maya Angelou and Janet Jackson to stop bullying and teen suicide.

He is a graduate of both Morehouse College and the University of Michigan where he was one of the youngest African-Americans to receive his PhD in Clinical Psychology. Dr. Tartt owns a thriving positive psychology practice in Decatur, GA and has successfully worked with well over a thousand clients in Georgia, California, and Michigan. He has served on the Board of Directors for the 100 Black Men of DeKalb and Forever Family. Dr. Tartt is also an associate member of the National Speakers Association of Georgia.

Give the Gift of

THE RING FORMULA:

How to be the Only *One* He Ever Needs

Dr. Alduan Tartt's

Go Online to ask your personal dating and relationship questions now!

For information about Dr. Alduan Tartt's presentations, book signings, products and wildly popular panel discussions and meet-ups or to order additional books and products, please visit his website and interact with him live at:

WWW.DRTARTT.COM

Or call:

(404) 377-4757

For bookings, speaking engagements, media interviews, and advice.

BOOK ME TO SPEAK

AT YOUR NEXT CONFERENCE, MEETING, GALA, ETC.

CALL ME NOW

404-377-4757

EMAIL: DRTARTT@DRTARTT.COM

JOIN MY EMAIL LIST AT

WESBITES: WWW.DRTARTT.COM & WWW.RINGFORMULA.COM

TWITTER: @DRTARTT

CPSIA information can be obtained at www.ICGtesting.com
Printed in the USA
BVOW09s0016051214

377534BV00003BA/104/P